ALSO BY SUE HUBBELL

A Book of Bees

A Country Year

On This Hilltop

Broadsides from the Other Orders

FAR-FLUNG HUBBELL

S U E *H U B B E L L*

Far-Flung Hubbell

RANDOM HOUSE

NEW YORK

Library of Congress Cataloging-in-Publication Data
Hubbell, Sue.
Far-flung Hubbell / Sue Hubbell.—1st ed.
p.   cm.
ISBN 0-679-42833-X
I. Title.
AC8.H89   1995   081—dc20   94-20309

Manufactured in the United States of America on
acid-free paper
Book design by J. K. Lambert
9 8 7 6 5 4 3 2
First Edition

for other mountains
for other views

Many of the pieces in this book were written for *The New Yorker* when I was a regular contributor under Bob Gottlieb's editorship. If Bob assigned an article to the department called "Our Far-Flung Correspondents," my working galleys would come through with the heading "Far-Flung (Hubbell)." This amused me, and I cut out one such heading and taped it to the wall above my desk. It certainly described my life in those days. I have homes both in Missouri and Washington, D.C., and was driving the 1,010 miles between the two with frequency, but the truth was I was hardly ever in either place; more often I was out on the road working on one of the stories you'll find in this collection, or else gathering material for a book I was writing toward the end of those *New Yorker* years. Tazzie, the finest dog in the world, was usually curled up on the seat beside me, her head in my lap, and I notice that she has nuzzled her way into some of these pieces.

It was enormous fun. It was also fun to work for *The New Yorker,* which respected a writer's style and words above all. I recall one afternoon when I was to take a flight to Missouri; the magazine was closing the same day, and one of my pieces was in it. My editor was distressed that I would be out of telephone contact for a couple of hours and asked for a number at which she could leave a message. I gave her the number of the friend who was going to pick me up. When the plane landed, my friend, a little breathless, said, "Sue! Sue! You've got to contact *The New Yorker*! The woman who called said it was important." I dialed the number from a pay phone in the airport. My permission was being requested to change a "will not" to "won't" and a "did not" to "don't."

My regular editor at *The New Yorker* was Sarah Lippincott. First and foremost, an editor is a stand-in for the general reader, a person who can show the writer places where more explanation is needed or where she has been unclear. Having wallowed for months in her material, the writer may sometimes forget and make assumptions about knowledge that the reader may not have. Sarah fills this role magnificently, of course, but in addition she also has that mysterious ability common to the best editors, that of submerging her own sense of self and style into the writer's, and of being able to help a sentence in which the writer has not been true to herself. I would make a lousy editor because I am an egotist, irrevocably married to my own style, but Sarah has a selflessness and generosity that allows her to edit different writers without making them all sound the same. She is no longer at *The New Yorker*, but in those days I know that, in addition to me, she regularly edited Milton Viorst and John McPhee, two quite different writers, whose published work could never have been mistaken one for the other—least of all for mine.

But the great pleasure of those years was working for Bob Gottlieb. He approved or disallowed story ideas I turned in, read each piece as it was submitted, and read it again in final form before it went to press, occasionally noticing, even then, the one word that did not ring true or making some small suggestion that improved the piece. In discussing story ideas, Bob was quick and intuitive to see their potential. He could see the inherent humor, interest, and appeal in a situation, place, person, or event without it being spelled out, partly because he has enormous curiosity, wide interests, and an appreciative and gentle tolerance of what other people find interesting. Above all, he trusted and had faith in his writers. He assumed the best, and as a result brought out the best in them. He never tried to nudge a story, but had an uncanny skill of giving, if asked, the merest hint of advice that clarified a problem. The story in this collection that I found most difficult to write was "The Vicksburg Ghost." It is about a woman who sees Elvis Presley in the supermarket checkout line and is seized upon by a number of people who have agendas of their own. After I came home from Vicksburg I was having a hard time sorting out how I felt about the whole business. I talked to Bob and he said, "Keep it reportorial." That was all. It is a good piece of advice in any circumstance for a writer, but I needed to hear it just at that moment. I sat down and began writing.

Bob was enthusiastic when I turned in the idea for the Great American Pie Expedition; he is a good and serious pie eater. So during the months I was out on the road nibbling on one piece of pie after another, I would occasionally come across a kind that I thought deserved his attention and would send him a whole, freshly baked pie. The first arrival caused some commotion in the mailroom, but afterward the staff began to look forward to the shipments. In Virginia I found a restaurant that baked a mighty fine coconut-cream pie. This is Bob's favorite, but it is fragile, so the restaurant owner and a friendly truck driver who was headed to Manhattan worked out a deal whereby the driver was to put a coconut-cream pie on his front seat and deliver it personally. The pie never arrived. I guess the truck driver shared my opinion, and maybe this makes up for its loss to Bob and *The New Yorker* staff.

The Great American Pie Expedition piece, when written, included a number of recipes. *The New Yorker* fact-checking department was everything it was famous for and then some. Different fact checkers volunteered for different pies, baked them at home to make sure the recipes worked, and then brought them in to share. The piece I wrote about the magic convention ("Hey, Presto!") required a bit of fancy fact-checking, too, during the course of which Harry Blackstone, Jr., stopped by *The New Yorker* offices to demonstrate some of the tricks.

Those were good years.

On my kitchen shelf is a large jar of honey labeled OZARK MOUNTAIN WILDFLOWER HONEY, FROM THE HIVES OF SOLARIUS. Although the honey is amber and delicious, I have only occasionally tasted it over the years. I prefer to keep it as a talisman and a reminder. It reminds me of Sue Hubbell, which in turn recalls her lyrical descriptions of raising bees on her ninety-acre farm in the Ozarks. I am for a moment taken away from "the fever and the fret" of the city, from traffic and deadlines and news of foreign wars. The jar has richly served it purposes.

I first encountered Sue Hubbell's writing in 1984, when, as a harried editor at *The New York Times,* I was avoiding a rather large manuscript piled along with others in my office. When I came around to it, the account of starting over at age fifty after a divorce, broke, trying to establish a commercial honey operation, and living in a sod-floor cabin in the Ozarks immediately captivated me. A call to the author established that the pleasant, somewhat surprised person I was talking to was indeed real, and that she would be happy to try her hand at a series of "Hers" columns—essays of which I was editor that ran in the paper's Thursday Home Section at the time.

Sue Hubbell's columns appeared in New York between July and September 1984, and they created a small sensation. The phone rang, and rang. Who is the Bee Lady? Where can one buy her honey?, colleagues and readers, as well as Macy's Cellar, asked. Will she write for *us?* inquired fellow editors. Once discovered by a larger audience, Hubbell quickly went on to success: to date, she has had four books published and has written frequent articles for *Smithsonian* magazine and *The New Yorker,* among others.

Why the stir? Her dauntlessness in learning the skills of farm life from scratch explains in part the impact of those early essays. More important was her ability to evoke a vision of rural harmony for frazzled urban readers. Hubbell recounted the quiet pleasures and sometime hazards of beekeeping, she described the Ozarks in flowering spring and hazy autumn. Pastoral poets, especially ones who descend from the noble tradition of Virgil's *Georgics,* don't come along all that frequently, even if the scope, as here, is far more modest. Yet much of her writing is close to bucolic poetry.

A poet's sensibility is combined with a naturalist's eye, and Hubbell's keen scientific observations are the basis of two books, *The Book of Bees* and the recent *Broadsides from the Other Orders: A Book of Bugs.*

In this new volume, *Far-Flung,* an omnium-gatherum of Hubbell's articles and essays, her reportorial skills are brought to bear on a wide variety of subjects that take her away from her home ground in Missouri. Although she does manage to work in the great blue herons in the Federal Wildlife Refuge at Reelfoot, Missouri, and the only truck stop—the Carlisle All American in Pennsylvania—that is an officially designated crow roost, most of this book is devoted to people, Americans in their everyday lives and everyday, if often oddball, settings.

Rolling along U.S. Interstates in her three-quarter-ton pickup (used to deliver her annual honey crop), Hubbell pulls into truck stops from Maryland to Arizona, checking out the post office, shower room, fax machine, Laundromat, barbershop, travel store, and TV room (sometimes a full movie theater) of today's megafacility—along with the coffee at the restaurant and the service at the gas pumps. Not just an observer, Hubbell spends "truckerbucks," wears a MACK cap, and peruses *Road King Magazine* (lifetime subscription).

Coffee shops, truck stops, and cafés are her favorite listening posts. At Mar-Jo's in Vicksburg, Michigan, for instance, Hubbell finds out how many customers believe in the recent local "sightings" of Elvis Presley (none); in an exhaustive survey of pies in small roadside restaurants from Kentucky to Maine ("Never order pie in a restaurant within one mile of an interstate highway") she even includes recipes for the finest. Pies—banana-cream, lemon-meringue, apple, pecan, and blueberry, as well as regional eccentrics like peanut butter—inspire the precise analysis that is her trademark: "It was a trim, neat, light-brown wedge on a crisp crust, topped with daintily browned meringue" (this one from Buffalo Gap, Virginia, at the Our Place restaurant, a favorite).

In an impressive piece of reporting, Hubbell deflates the mythology of earthquake prediction, investigating the alarmist scenario projected from the New Madrid Seismic Zone in Missouri for 3 December 1990 by Iben Browning.

Hubbell reports on another world, that of magic and illusion, from The 53rd Annual Magic Get-Together in Colon, Michigan, where she spends the week with a thousand magicians. Of Harry Blackstone's performance with a freestanding light bulb, she writes:

He sends it, glowing, down to the front rows of the audience, where he invites spectators to touch it and reassure themselves of its substance. . . . Luminous, spectral, the bulb—a mere light bulb, made lovely and strange by behaving in a way that no mundane light bulb should—drifts gently out over the audience and then soars back to its master, who returns it to the lamp. And I understand that I have never really seen a light bulb before.

From the Florida newsroom of the scandal-flogging tabloids *Weekly World News* and *The Enquirer* to the Bowling Alley Hall of Fame in St. Louis, from the trucker to the piemaker to the citizens in a small-town café, Hubbell captures the eccentric in the everyday, taking us with her across America, grateful for the ride.

—*Nancy Newhouse*

CONTENTS

FAR-FLUNG HUBBELL

ONE

The Great American Pie Expedition

Nobody needs drug-store ice cream;
pie is good enough for anybody.

—*Sinclair Lewis,* Main Street

asy as pie. It's easy to make good, tasty, comforting, serviceable pie. Of course, excellent pie is harder to make, and harder to find, but excellence is always rare. The Shaker Lemon Pie served at Shaker Village of Pleasant Hill, near Harrodsburg, Kentucky, is an excellent pie. The Shakers invented this pie back in the early 1800s, when they began trading goods they grew or manufactured for the few necessities they couldn't produce. Lemons, which they considered an important item in a healthy diet, were one of the "world's goods" they needed. Their lemons came all the way from New Orleans and were so dear that the Shakers believed it a sin to waste any part of them, so they devised a recipe that would use the whole lemon.

Pie made from that recipe is served in the public dining room of the Trustees' House at Shaker Village. The pie has a beautifully browned crust—surprisingly thick, but so light and flaky that it shatters under a fork. Inside is a generous lemon custard, with bits of lemon pulp and rind throughout. The sourness of the lemon plays off the sweetness of the custard in an altogether delicious way. It is a pretty pie, too. Here is the way to make both the crust and the filling. The recipes are from *We Make You Kindly Welcome*, a cookbook available at the restaurant.

CRUST FOR A 9-INCH PIE

2 cups flour	*⅔ cup plus 4 tbsp.*
1 tsp. salt	*shortening*
	4 tbsp. cold water

Mix flour and salt. Cut shortening into flour until it forms very small balls. Sprinkle in water, a tbsp. at a time, while mixing lightly with a fork until the flour is moistened. Mix it into a ball that cleans the bowl. Do not overwork the dough. Roll out on floured board.

(The less you handle dough, the better; handling toughens it. A good crust must be crisp, even at the risk of being a bit crumbly.)

SHAKER LEMON PIE

2 large lemons with	*4 eggs, well beaten*
very thin rinds	*Crust for pie*
2 cups sugar	

Slice lemons as thin as paper, rind and all. Combine with sugar; mix well. Let stand 2 hours, or preferably overnight, blending occasionally. Add beaten eggs to lemon mixture; mix well. Turn into 9-inch pie shell, arranging lemon slices evenly. Cover with top crust. Cut several slits near center. Bake at 450° for 15 minutes. Reduce heat to 375° and bake for about 20 minutes or until silver knife inserted near edge of pie comes out clean. Cool before serving.

Pleasant Hill is on U.S. 68, the Harrodsburg Road, which winds past prosperous-looking horse farms, curving through stratified rock as it dips down to cross the Kentucky River. There have been no Shakers at Shaker Village since 1923, but it has been restored to its bucolic picturesqueness. After eating the excellent lemon pie, I went back to my car and let my dog, Tazzie, out for a run. We found a sheepy hillside and sprawled out on it, soaking up the early spring sunshine. Tazzie, who is mostly German shepherd but with soft edges, gazed decorously at the sheep, sniffed the air, and rolled over on her back in the short grass, kicking her feet lazily in the air. I lay on my back, too, staring at fluffy clouds and listening to meadowlarks.

My family has always been a pie family. When my son, Brian, was in high school, he spent more time hitchhiking around the country with friends than I or those in loco parentis at his boarding school ever knew. He and his friends seldom had much money, but they always had enough in their jeans to buy pie and coffee. Fifteen years and more later, he is still an expert on pie in astonishing places. A few years ago, I was driving across the country with him and his wife, Liddy, when, in a small town in Kentucky, an abstracted look came across his face. He said to Liddy, who was driving, "If you'll turn left at the stop sign and then go two blocks, there's a place that has really good pecan pie." We did, and there was. We sat there eating pie and drinking coffee, and, caffeine coursing through our veins, we spun a plan. Someday we would drive around the country on back roads and eat pie. It would be the Great American Pie Expedition. Their lives, alas, are now regulated by jobs, but mine grows freer and more unruly with each passing year, so Tazzie and I had undertaken the pie expedition. We were on its final leg; during the previous summer and autumn, we had been eating pie—some good, some bad, some indifferent—through Pennsylvania, southern New England, and on into Maine, where the blueberry and raspberry pies are glorious. Now we were heading west, through the cream-pie belt.

Before setting out on the initial trip that summer, I had wanted to establish some sort of standard for the expedition—a federal benchmark. I was in Washington, D.C., where I live for part of the year, so my husband and I went to lunch at the United States Senate Family Dining Room, which prides itself on its pie—particularly its pecan pie—nearly as much as it does on its bean soup. It seemed our patriotic duty to order, in addition to the pecan, the Senate Apple Pie, and only fair to add the special of the day, Senate Chocolate Mousse Pie. The last-named turned out to be a triumph of the imitation-food industry, and the apple pie was more government issue than federal benchmark. Both it and the pecan had been warmed up, though not, thank heaven, in a microwave oven. The microwave oven is one of the worst enemies that pie has in restaurant kitchens these days. I remember especially a piece of raspberry pie in Maine that had been microwaved to death. The hot raspberries, all integrity gone, oozed sadly out of the crust, and the pie had a faintly bitter aftertaste. Freshly made, warm pie is one of life's better things, but after it cools it should be allowed to grow old gently rather than brought back to an unnatural warmth. Our government-issue apple pie was no worse than many apple pies I was to sample on the road, but certainly no better. It contained too much cornstarch filling and too few apples, and those present were flaccid and tasteless. The pecan was a marginal improvement, but so cloying that it would have benefited from the quarter cup of brandy a friend of mine always adds to pecan-pie filling to cut its sweetness.

A few days later, Tazzie and I headed west and north in search of better pie. In western Maryland, on U.S. 40 at Sideling Hill, we drove through a magnificent roadcut, which is sometimes shown in geology textbooks; it is a place where a great part of the earth's history is laid out. There are signs along the roadside: NO PARKING. NO CLIMBING. No gawking, no looking, don't be interested in what there is to see. When I had driven through there with Brian and Liddy on our trip a few years back, the State of Maryland wasn't so prohibitive, and we had parked, climbed, gawked.

Tazzie and I followed U.S. 40 north into Pennsylvania, stopping by the bank of a stream for Tazzie to run and for me to have a cup of coffee from the thermos. It was June, and the cow parsnip would soon be in bloom; daisies and buttercups already were. Wild geranium was everywhere. A blackbird, pert and sweet-voiced, was singing. "There's a cabbage white," I told Tazzie, "and there's a tiger swallowtail." I was trying to interest her in butterflies, but she paid them no attention whatever.

I sat sipping my coffee and thinking about pie. Meat pies, according to *The Columbia Encyclopedia,* have been around since the days of the Romans, but no one mentions fruit pies—or any dessert pies—until the fifteenth century. Even after that, no one ate very much pie until the New World was settled. Americans were the first to understand what pie could be. For instance, the English had been making what they called pompion by cutting a hole in the side of a pumpkin, extracting the seeds and the filaments, stuffing the cavity with apples, and baking the whole. New Englanders improved on this, combining the apples and pumpkin and putting them in a proper pastry. Then they eliminated the apples and added milk, eggs, spices, and molasses to the mashed, stewed pumpkin. Molasses, the colonists' substitute for sugar, was so important for pies that on several occasions a New England town put off its celebration of Thanksgiving for a week or more in anticipation of a shipment of molasses from the West Indies.

Americans discovered that other tasty pies could be made from materials at hand. A mock-cherry pie could be made with Cape Cod cranberries (spiced with raisins from Spain). Vermont pie was made with apples—a fruit successfully transplanted from England—and syrup cooked down from the sap of maple trees. Pie has never been more loved than in nineteenth-century America, where it was not simply dessert but also a normal part of breakfast. The food writer Evan Jones quotes a contemporary observer as noting that in northern New England "all the hill and country towns were full of women who would be mortified if visitors caught them without pie in the house," and that the absence of pie at breakfast "was more noticeable than the scarcity of the Bible." I knew a farmer in Iowa who died at the age of ninety-three a contented man, for he had eaten pie at breakfast every day of his life.

Herrings Family Restaurant is on U.S. 40—on the eastern outskirts of Uniontown, Pennsylvania. It is called a family restaurant not because it is O.K. to wear blue jeans there or because the food is moderately priced (although both these things are true) but because the Herring family runs it. I sat in a rosy-orange plastic booth and had a home-style platter of beef stew, and after eating it I hoped that the pies would be as good. There was a choice: banana, coconut, peanut-butter, lemon, cherry-cream, blackberry, apple, cherry, raisin, and peach. A friend had recommended the banana pie, so I ordered that, but I couldn't resist ordering blackberry, too. The waitress looked amused. "I never had anyone order two pieces of pie before," she said. The crust on both pies was superb. The banana was still a little warm, and the filling spilled onto the plate. The bananas had been mashed before cooking, so there was pulp throughout instead of discrete slices. It was a good pie, but the blackberry was even better—tart and beautifully seedy. It was dense with fruit and had just as much filler as was needed, no more. The maker of the pies was pointed out to me—a slim, bespectacled young man. He blushed when I congratulated him on his pie-baking abilities, and told me that he sometimes made the pies but his relatives also made them. "The whole family works at the business," he said. "Grandpap started it. We all work in it." He pointed to the waitress. "She's my cousin."

"We make pies every day," his cousin said as I paid my check. "Doughnuts, too. And bread. And we eat all of them, but we stay skinny."

In the days that followed, I remembered fondly the pie at Herrings, for I had pies so middling as to be not worth reporting and one that was bad enough to be notable. I would not have been cross about this particular peach pie if pie had not been so boasted of on the restaurant's menu, and if it had not been peach season. I had asked for the apricot pie, which I'd heard good things about, but apricot was not available the day I was there, and since it was the height of the peach harvest I didn't think I could go wrong ordering peach pie. The crust was tasteless and thick and rested heavily in the stomach. The cook had been stingy with the peaches, which were suspended in a gluelike filling. I've had bad peach pie *out* of season—I remember especially one canned-peach pie in El Reno, Oklahoma—but during peach season it is hard not to make a good peach pie. Fresh peaches should be sliced and sweetened with enough white or brown sugar to make them pleasant to the taste. Egg yolk mixed with flour is a good thickener for peach pie, and after the thickener, sugar, and peaches have been lightly combined they should be heaped up roundly in an unbaked shell, topped with more crust, and baked. Toward the end of the baking, the pie should be removed briefly from the oven and the top crust brushed with a bit of egg white and sprinkled with sugar and cinnamon; the pie is then returned to the oven to brown prettily. That's all there is to it.

Of course, the underpinning of that pie—the crust—should be adequate. A New York man I know who thinks about pie a great deal says that pie judgments are sexually dimorphic. He believes that women judge a pie by its crust, men by its filling. That's so, says my friend Abby, because women know that the crust is the hardest part to make. That's *not* so, says my friend Linda, who loves both parts too much but eats only the filling, in the vain hope that most of the calories have settled in the crust. The truth is that a good pie can be ruined by a bad crust but a good crust cannot save a bad pie. A crust can be only so good, anyway. It should show off the pie and not call a lot of attention to itself. On my pie expedition I often found that restaurant cooks used frozen pie shells rather than making crusts themselves. In many cases, that was probably a mercy, because if left to their own devices they would make worse. Once, after I had eaten a memorably bad piece of cherry pie in a café in West Virginia, the cook and the waitress sat down in my booth to talk. I asked the cook how she made the crust, which was thick and soggy. She told me that it was made of Crisco, flour, and milk. I've had a few bad milk crusts, and I don't use milk myself. Seldom has there been a week in my adult life when I haven't made a pie, and the following is the crust I use more often than any other. It is easy to make, crisp in a way that flakier crusts can't be, and shows off many pie fillings to advantage.

DOUGH FOR A 2-CRUST PIE

2 cups flour	¼ cup water
1 tsp. salt	½ cup cooking oil

Mix flour and salt in a bowl and make a hollow in center of the mixture. Rapidly blend water and oil together in a cup and pour into hollow in flour-salt mixture. Combine ingredients quickly and lightly with a few strokes of a spoon. Pinch dough in half and roll out each half between two sheets of waxed paper. Peel off top layer of paper. Invert dough into piepan and remove second layer of waxed paper.

On several occasions in the course of my expedition I stopped at the Mount Nittany Inn, which is just north of Tusseyville on Pennsylvania Route 144, hoping to have its special peanut-butter pie. A man whose pie sense I trust had urged me to try it. "Just don't think about it too much," he said. "Once you get over the idea of it, it's really terrific." But each time I went there the peanut-butter pie was not available, for one reason or another. The inn's proprietor agreed that it was a wonderful pie; his wife made it, he told me, but he didn't know how. "She makes the peanut butter all creamy, and then she freezes it," he said. "But I don't know what all she puts into it. A lot of stuff. Cheese, maybe?" I do hope not. In an effort not to think about *that*, I finally ordered, on my third stop, the inn's walnut pie, which was very good indeed. The crust was perfect, and the filling was similar to that of a good pecan pie, with black walnuts substituted for the pecans. The whole was topped with cream, whipped gently. It was satisfying, but not satisfying enough to drive the peanut-butter pie from my mind. I wish I could stop thinking about it.

I also failed to have the famous sour-cream raisin pie at the Potato City Motor Inn, in Potter County, Pennsylvania. That harsh, empty country, on the northern edge of the state, comes into its own in winter, during hunting and snow seasons. In daisy time, the Potato City Motor Inn is a quiet, unvisited place and serves up no sour-cream raisin pie. I asked the waitress which of the three pies available that day I should order. "None of 'em," she said. The Potato City Motor Inn was originally built as a place for potato growers to meet. Dr. E. L. Nixon, uncle to Himself, was involved in the beginnings of Potato City, where he crossbred potatoes and developed new strains. The cavernous dining rooms of the inn were empty when I was there. I would have liked at least to see the nearby ice mine, "a deep mountainside shaft" that "for no apparent reason forms heavy ice beginning in the spring," according to my Pennsylvania road map, which adds, "In winter the ice disappears." But it was closed. Potter County was in commercial diapause, so we drove on.

I stopped to feed Tazzie in a spruce woods, where bracken grew among the trees. While she ate, I watched clouds of blue butterflies— spring azures—squeezing into nearly opened blackberry blossoms to lay their eggs. We drove east on U.S. 6, a gentle road that wound through small towns filled with well-kept, late-nineteenth-century houses surrounded by poppies. In between towns, wild blue phlox and buttercups

were in bloom. I heard an Eastern wood pewee calling *pee-a-weeee,
peee-a-wee*. But the pie was indifferent until the X-Trail Restaurant, in
Mansfield, at the intersection of U.S. 6 and Business Route U.S. 15. The
X-Trail is a cheerful, unpretentious restaurant, painted blue, with crisp
blue-and-white curtains at mullioned windows. It serves good pie baked
in deep-dish piepans, which is just the way pies should be baked. (These
pans are hard to find—something I discovered while shopping for one
as a birthday present for Michael, my stepson, who has become interested in piemaking. But a few stores still stock them, and any serious
piemaker should have one.) The X-Trail's coconut-cream pie was cool
enough to cut, so I ordered some. It was a delicate pie, a handsome
pie—monochrome, with white meringue floating on a cream-white
filling whose very pallor guaranteed that no packaged mix had been
used. The crust was crisp, clean, distinct. The waitress told me that it
was the restaurant's most favored pie—even more popular than the
black-raspberry pie, which I also sampled, and which was stuffed with
juicy berries.

I asked at each of my stops which pie was the most popular, and
usually it was the coconut-cream. Coconut-cream is a good year-round
pie. My friend Charlie, a Republican, is a pie conservative, and he
doesn't believe in cream pies. The only real pies, he says, are of berries
or other fruit, but he thinks that no one makes even fruit pies very well
anymore. "You're not going to find good apple pie anywhere," he told
me. I hoped he was wrong, but as the summer progressed it seemed
possible that he might not be. When in doubt, I always ordered apple
pie, and it was almost always as bad as the government-issue pie I'd had
back in Washington—or worse. With such a standard, small wonder that
gardeners with a lot of green tomatoes on their hands at the end of the
season and with frost imminent tell us that green-tomato pie is just as
good as apple any day.

Charlie wouldn't have approved of the chocolate-meringue pie I had at the Hotel Wyalusing, in Wyalusing, Pennsylvania, just off U.S. 6, by the Susquehanna River. I did. It was made of bittersweet chocolate so rich that the memory of Droste chocolate apples came to me. The meringue was as brown as a toasted marshmallow and so flat and neat that it must have been spread with a knife. I would have enjoyed staying at the Hotel Wyalusing. It was a pleasant place—a former stagecoach stop lovingly restored, its brick front cleaned and its gingerbread wood-work, balconies, and dormers painted pale olive and buff yellow—but I wanted to eat pie at a New Jersey diner, and I wanted to get on to New York City to pick up a sweet-potato pie from Hugh Nelms, the president and corn-breadist of Hoecake International, so I drove on.

I discovered on my pie expedition that making a schedule was often a mistake. Certainly it was this time, because twenty-five miles west of New York City a tractor-trailer rig had tumbled over, and as a result all of northern New Jersey was in gridlock. I coasted, usually in neutral, across the state, reading the *Times* from page one through the classifieds, seldom passing the one-mile-per-hour mark. Pie at a diner was the first part of the plan to be abandoned, but I did want that sweet-potato pie. Abby had been telling me about it for years. She said that Nelms sells his pie every Sunday in fine weather at the open-air market at Seventy-seventh Street and Columbus Avenue. It is, she told me, a beautiful pie to look at, and a pie so tasty that she can't resist buying it in the six-inch-wide, hand-held version and eating it on the spot.

I tried to break away to the north, thinking I might come into the city from a different direction, but there had been a two-car collision some-where in Connecticut, and that made the northern roads sluggish, too. Pie thoughts faded, and all I could think of was escape. I fled to the wilds of western Massachusetts and took stock. Sweet-potato pie would have to be added to my list of pies not sampled: Nittany peanut-butter, sour-cream raisin, apricot, sweet-potato. I don't like shoofly pie—a pie that has always reminded me of sweetened library paste—and wasn't even going to try eating that. I do like Key lime, but Florida was not on my route. Nor was Colorado, though a friend had recommended the black-bottom pie in Denver. Nor Wisconsin, where there was said to be a strawberry pie so good that it was impossible to eat only one piece.

The next day was better. It was a golden, sunny morning, and beside the Connecticut River at Turners Falls, Massachusetts, I stopped in a park filled with bluebells to give Tazzie a short run. A friendly woman was walking her dog, who was part hound, part black Lab, and Tazzie fell in love with him. While our dogs played, the woman and I talked, and she told me about the Shady Glen, a restaurant on the main street of Turners Falls, where a friend of hers went once a day to eat chocolate-cream pie. The Shady Glen is a wide, squat, hospitable café. Inside are cheerful yellow booths and a wide selection of pies. I ordered the squash pie. It was my first of the season, nicely spiced with nutmeg and set off by a firm, crisp crust.

Diner chic is spreading, but it has not yet come to the Miss Florence Diner, on State Route 9, in Florence, Massachusetts, a vestigial outcropping of the more uptown-looking Alexander's Taproom. Miss Florence appears to have been there a long time and looks as though it would outlast Alexander's. It serves a thick, sincere apple pie—not an exceptional pie but a good pie. The apple pie at Allen Brothers Farm Market, on U.S. 5, in Westminster, Vermont, *is* exceptional. The indoor farm stand smelled of good things from the bakery the day I was there, but the fragrance of fresh apple pies dominated all. ("Thy breath is like the steame of apple-pyes," Robert Greene wrote in 1589.) I bought a whole one and a slab of Vermont Cheddar to go with it, and then I drove down to Boston, where I was going to meet my husband and stay with Brian and Liddy, who live there.

It was an apple pie almost beyond praise. "This pie is good enough for breakfast," Liddy said reverently. The crust set it off well, and the apples—Lodis, in this case—were superb. Some of their skins had escaped the peeler and were in the pie, an addition that the four of us liked, but when I talked later to Alice Porter, the Allens' baker, she was a bit embarrassed about them. Tim Allen, a second-generation apple grower, says Northern Spies make the best apple pie, and that's the variety Mrs. Porter uses when they're in season. When they're not, she uses Lodis or Cortlands.

ALLENS' PIECRUST

2 cups flour	*1 egg*
1½ tsp. sugar	*1 tbsp. vinegar*
1 tsp. salt	*¼ cup water*
¾ cup shortening	

Mix dry ingredients in a bowl and cut in shortening with a pastry blender. In a separate bowl beat together egg, vinegar, and water. Mix with dry ingredients and refrigerate dough for at least two hours before rolling out. Makes a 9-inch two-crust pie.

ALLENS' APPLE-PIE FILLING

2 tbsp. flour	*½ tsp. cinnamon*
½ to ¾ cup sugar,	*¼ tsp. nutmeg*
depending upon	*4 cups sliced apples*
tartness of apples	

Mix flour, sugar, and spices. Add to apples and mix lightly. Pour into unbaked pie shell. Dot with butter. Cover with top crust. Brush top with whole egg beaten with a little milk. Bake at 325° for 35 to 40 minutes or until browned.

Charlie, there's your pie.

In Maine, I settled into a routine of raspberry and blueberry pie, and each one was better than the one before it, which makes them very difficult to write about. The raspberry I remember with the greatest fondness is one I bought at the Village One Stop, in Lovell, in the western part of the state. One stop indeed: liquor, worms, gas, grain, groceries, lunch counter. A sign over the lunch counter, hand-lettered, said PLEASE EAT OR WE'LL BOTH STARVE. I asked the young woman behind the counter about pie. She pointed to a man in a plaid flannel shirt sitting on a stool at the far end. "Talk to him—he just finished baking them."

"You have pie?" I asked him.

"Yep."

"What kind?"

"Pineapple. Blackberry. Raspberry."

"Raspberry sounds good."

Silence.

"May I have some?"

"Well . . . They're awful warm to cut. You want a whole pie?"

"Please."

The whole pie was five dollars and eighty-five cents. I bought it and a copy of *The Boston Globe*. The man smiled, faintly, and said, "Have a nice one. I mean a day, I guess. Have a nice day."

The warm pie filled the car with its fragrance. Tazzie and I drove north on State Route 5. The bracken at the roadside had the hint of bronze that says fall is on its way. The air and the sunlight agreed. We threaded in and out among logging trucks and finally pulled in at a rest stop, beside a lake where a loon was calling. A handcarved sign on a post said that the spot was not maintained by any government agency and asked me to take away my trash. A reasonable request. The entreaty was signed by E. Littlefield—presumably the person who had mowed the grass so neatly and painted the blue picnic table, which was sheltered by a maple tree. Tazzie checked out the lakeshore, and I joined her, balancing on the rocks there. The late-morning sun made the wavelets glisten, their shimmer set off by the dark greens of spruce, fir, and pine that ringed the lake. I spread my *Globe* out on the picnic table, poured coffee from my thermos, and took out the pie. It was nicely browned and had little slash marks in the crust to let the steam escape. The edges were lovingly crimped, and the crust broke apart under my fork in delicious shattery flakes. The filling was no sweeter than it needed to be. It tasted of fresh raspberries and summer sunshine. I read my *Globe* and listened to the loon and ate pie. Thank you, E. Littlefield.

We resumed our drive north, but the blue sky and the sunshine prompted us to stop beside the Sunday River. Tazzie made friends with a man in sweatshirt and jeans who was peering at trees in a puzzled way. He asked if I had a field guide to trees with me. I did. We talked trees, and he told me that he had just begun learning to identify trees and birds and was driving around the country trying to learn the names of all he saw. Splendid man. I asked him if he'd like five-sixths of a really good raspberry pie. He said yes, and I gave it to him.

One afternoon, we stopped beside the Kennebec River, below the town of Skowhegan and its falls. Tazzie pounced on crickets, catching none. I watched damselflies. Clouds thickened and turned gray as they floated up from the southwest. Goldenrod and aster, the yellow and purple of summer's end, bloomed around us. I could hear a chain saw somewhere. All along the roads I'd been driving, I'd seen serious, multicord woodpiles. Winter is never far from the thoughts of people who live in north country.

Tazzie, who takes more interest in rocks than most dogs do, and certainly more than is good for her teeth, fetched numbers of them out of the Kennebec and laid them neatly on the bank, sometimes sticking her entire head underwater in a most undoglike fashion. We drove on through towns whose front lawns were bright with mountain ash, through Passadumkeag, through Mattawamkeag—which is to say that we were on our way to Aroostook, or The County, as Down Easters call it. And there, in Houlton, I found the Elm Tree Diner, on the southwestern edge of town, on U.S. Alternate 2. It specialized in homemade pies, and it was a busy place, with table-filled additions that were signs of its commercial success. The blueberry pie had a thick but light crust. The berries were sparingly sweetened and little cooked; they maintained their integrity and berryish freshness so well that they brought back the memory of a sunny day when Brian, then twelve, and his father and I walked up Cadillac Mountain and stuffed ourselves with blueberries that we picked as we climbed.

I would have liked to buy pie in Wytopitlock, but there was none to be had, so I stopped in front of a boarded-up general store (FOR SALE), amid an unkempt patch of orange hawkweed, red clover, and pesky ripe burdock waiting for a chance to entangle itself in Tazzie's fur. There I ate a piece of French apple pie that I'd had the foresight to buy at the Elm Tree Diner. It is the same pie that in Pennsylvania is called Dutch apple pie—a single-crust apple pie topped with a crumbly mixture of brown sugar, flour, and butter (the "dowdy" of apple pan-dowdy). This French apple, however, was much better than any of its Pennsylvania Dutch relatives that I had sampled. It was generously filled with apples, and was pleasantly tart. It is always a mistake to sweeten these pies much, because the crumbly dowdy is sweet enough, and needs the sharp fruit contrast to be at its best.

Never play cards with a man named Doc, never eat at a place called Mom's, and never go to bed with anyone who has more troubles than you do, Nelson Algren advised. I discovered an exception in the case of a place called Mom's on U.S. 1, in Harrington, where I met Liddy and Brian for a traveling pie party. We ordered strawberry-rhubarb, apple, and blueberry pies and shared them. The strawberry-rhubarb was out of season but good nevertheless, and the apple was good, too, with a lovely ooze-browned back to its crust. The blueberry was the best I'd had so far. The crust was good—thick but not heavy—and the fresh blueberries that filled it were wild ones, sparkling and tangy. And then there was the blueberry pie we had at Duffy's, in East Orland, which was the last one I ate and the best one of all. The legend on the cover of Duffy's menu sounds a bit truculent:

WELCOME TO DUFFY'S

WE HERE AT DUFFY'S ARE A

NATIVE ORIENTATED RESTAURANT

WE AREN'T FUSSY

AND WE'RE CERTAINLY NOT FANCY.

IF YOU ARE,

ELLSWORTH IS 12 MILES EAST

AND

BUCKSPORT IS 7 MILES WEST.

YOURS TRULY,

DUFFY

Even so, Duffy's is a welcoming sort of place, with geranium-filled window boxes. We ordered graham-cracker pie first. "You know what banana-cream pie is?" the waitress asked. "Well, it's like that, without the bananas." That's not quite accurate. It was more like a custard pie on a graham-cracker crust, topped with whipped cream and sprinkled with graham-cracker crumbs. Quite good, and much better than most custard pies, which are at best sweet, modest little things. But the three of us gave the blueberry pie gold stars all around. The crust had been pinched up into extreme points, and was delicious. The local blueberries were delicious, too, and their flavor was enhanced by the generous addition of cinnamon.

In season, though, all blueberry pies are good. A few years ago, I was visiting a nonbaking friend, who asked me to make one. The oven wasn't working, but we thought we might be able to bake it on the covered outdoor grill, over a wood fire. There was no piepan, but perhaps I could make do with an aluminum cake pan. There was no rolling pin or waxed paper, so I used a water glass to roll out the pie dough between two pieces of brown paper cut from a grocery bag. There were, however, plenty of fresh wild blueberries, and there was sugar and cinnamon and a lemon, which I cut up and added to the filling. The pie that came off the grill had rather too thick a crust, and it had cooked unevenly, and it tasted of wood smoke, but it wasn't a *bad* pie; the blueberries were too good for that.

I had two other pies of note in Maine. The Farmington Diner, under the sign of fork and spoon transverse, was on State Route 4, on the south side of Farmington; it laid out logger-sized meals and good pie. The lunch special the day I was there was two thick pork chops cut from a very large pig, a platter of carrots, a platter of mashed potatoes and gravy, and a soup bowl full of applesauce. I made tiny inroads on the food, and realizing that I'd badly neglected lemon-meringue pie I ordered a wedge of it. It came accompanied by coffee in a sturdy mug that fitted amiably into my hand. My eyes told me that the pie filling was too yellow to be anything but a mix, but my taste buds said they didn't care: it was a good, classic diner pie—lots of loft to the meringue, and the crust a bit relaxed. Real lemon-meringue pie is too delicate and too ephemeral to be served in a diner, and too fussy to make for a diner cook to be happy with it.

The Milbridge House, in Milbridge, near the intersection of U.S. 1 and U.S. Alternate 1, serves a tasty and unusual pie. It is called Nantucket Cranberry Pie, and the recipe was brought up to Maine by Greg Charczuk, who owns the restaurant, when he moved from New Jersey. I copied it from the stained scrap of paper that his wife, Helen, uses when she makes it.

NANTUCKET CRANBERRY PIE

3 cups fresh cranberries	*1¼ tsp. baking powder*
Sugar to coat berries	*⅛ tsp. salt*
½ cup chopped walnuts	*1 egg*
¼ cup shortening	*⅓ cup milk*
1 cup sugar	*½ tsp. vanilla*
1 cup flour	*⅛ tsp. almond extract*

Rinse cranberries, and dredge with sugar. Pour into greased 10-inch piepan, leaving excess sugar in bowl. Add chopped walnuts to cranberries. Cream shortening with 1 cup sugar. Add dry ingredients alternately with mixture of egg, milk, vanilla, and almond. Spoon and spread over cranberries and walnuts. Bake at 350° for 25 to 30 minutes.

This is a fine pie, but, because the crust is cakelike and all on top, there will be pie conservatives who won't accept it. I will. If a creative and artful cook invents something and calls it pie, I'll call it pie. Let the crabbed formalists make their categories; I wouldn't like to miss something as lovely as this cranberry-walnut pie—an echo of the colonists' mock-cherry—or the banana-puddin' pie, which will make its appearance later.

My autumn was a busy one, and then the snows came, so it wasn't until the highways cleared in early springtime that Tazzie and I headed south from Washington on the pie roads.

Just south of Buffalo Gap, Virginia, on State Route 42, I came upon Our Place. It was part house, part restaurant, and was presided over by Betty Wade, a blond, comfortable woman with an easy smile. She showed me the back living room, where her daughters used to play until they were old enough to help out in the restaurant. Thirteen years ago, she told me, she and her husband bought the restaurant, and she started cooking there using *The Better Homes and Gardens Cook Book,* just as she did at home. "I wasn't sure folks would like my cooking," she said. "But they did. I didn't have to change anything." It seemed like the right kind of place to order butterscotch pie. I did, and watched the waitress slip quarters into the Wurlitzer.

> Shoe string, you ain't got no
>   money.
> Shoe string, you cain't hang
>   around here.
> Shoe string, you got your hat on
>   back'ards.

My pie arrived. It was a trim, neat, light-brown wedge on a crisp crust, topped with daintily browned meringue. Home cooking: I am back in the nineteen-forties, hungry as only an eight-year-old can be with supper still half an hour away. I am standing in front of the open door of a refrigerator—a big one, with gently sloping shoulders. Inside, on the shelf next to the ice-cube-tray compartment, is a row of tall stemmed dessert glasses, each one filled with its own golden dollop of butterscotch pudding. I count. There are five, and five of us will sit down to supper. There is no way I can winkle one out of the refrigerator without drawing down maternal wrath. I can't remember what happened after that. I can't even remember eating the butterscotch pudding after finishing my nice vegetables. All I can remember is the yearning. I'm glad to be an adult. As I leave, George Jones is wailing from the Wurlitzer:

> The last thing I gave her was
>   the bird,
> And she returned the favor with
>   a few selected words.

We drove on. State Route 42 is my kind of road, playing tag with a little river that glistened in the sunlight. Well-tended farms are tucked in among the hills. We stopped at a wayside, superior in every respect to interstate rest stops, and Tazzie ran about, sampling the river, snuffling expectantly at the newly softened ground. A nuthatch in a sycamore at the river edge called *whoink . . . whoink* as he surveyed the bark for edibles. I leaned against the same tree and soaked up the wan sunshine, glad to be on the road, glad to be driving south to meet the springtime.

Pie called, and we got back in the car and went west on U.S. 60, a more peaceable road than the distant but parallel interstate. In Grayson, Kentucky, on Main Street, I stopped at the City Café, in accordance with pie rules I have formulated over the years for the Middle West. Rule 1: Pie is good in 85 percent of the eating establishments that are between two other buildings. Rule 2: Good pie may often be had near places where meadowlarks sing. If you follow these two rules in the Middle West you will find yourself at the City Café or its like. A restaurant like this makes it unnecessary for a town to have anything but a bland local newspaper. Nearly all the citizens gather there early in the morning for breakfast or coffee and the exchange of news and gossip. By 8:30 A.M., whatever has happened during the past twenty-four hours has been talked over. These cafés have a pressed-metal ceiling, sometimes covered with insulating panels, and dark imitation-wood paneling on the walls. Oil paintings by local artists are often displayed there for sale. The doors open early—by five or five-thirty. Fresh-baked pie is ready by nine-thirty or ten. The coffee drinkers are replaced by the dinner crowd not long after (away from cities, dinner is the noontime meal), and by two the pie is gone and the restaurant is closed for the day.

There was a Mountain Dew sign in front of the City Café. A poster in the window promoted a local wrestling match. Inside were an imitation-brick carpet and imitation-woodgrain tables. Everything was imitation except the food. I ordered pecan pie. It was exceptional—solid, with good texture. The filling was rich and eggy tasting but not overpoweringly sweet. The pecans on top were chopped, glazed, brown. Wilma Berry, a big woman with a pleasant face and a curly hairdo, was the waitress and owner of the café. She was happy to share her recipe, adapted from *What's Cooking in Kentucky:*

PALESTENE LAYNE'S PECAN PIE

1 tsp. vanilla
3 eggs, slightly beaten
1 cup corn syrup,
   light or dark
½ tsp. salt
½ cup white sugar

½ cup brown sugar
2 cups coarsely
   chopped pecans
1 unbaked 9-inch,
   deep-dish pie shell

Blend well, but do not overbeat, vanilla, eggs, corn syrup, salt, sugar. Stir in pecans. Pour into pie shell. Bake approximately 50 minutes in preheated 350° oven, or until knife comes out clean.

The Beaver Dam Café was on the main street of Beaver Dam, Kentucky, just off U.S. 231, and was nestled between the Style Shop and Catalyst Management, Ltd. The sign outside said HOME OF GOOD FOOD. Inside, imitation-needlepoint placemats said:

CHERISH YESTERDAY

DREAM OF TOMORROW

LIVE TODAY

Nice, I thought; the Beaver Dam Café would have good pie. The possibilities, according to the menu, were interesting: cherry, pinto-bean, pecan, banana-pudding, and (Sundays only) buttermilk. It wasn't Sunday, nor was the pinto-bean ready, so I asked the waitress what I should order. "We sure do brag on our banana-puddin' pie," she said. I ordered banana-puddin' pie. It was fresh from the kitchen, chock-full of bananas, and so warm and relaxed that it had to be served in a bowl. The manager—a birdlike, wary little woman—said she'd be happy to give me the recipe but not her name. "What if someone tried to make it and didn't like it?" she asked. I am able to reassure her. Over the past months, my stepson has been committing pie courtship. He and his friend Barbara have been having pie dates, making pies from the recipes I brought back from my expedition. They tell me that the pecan and apple pies were the best all around and Shaker lemon the prettiest and most flavorful, but that the banana-puddin' pie was the most fun.

BEAVER DAM CAFÉ BANANA-PUDDIN' PIE

4 eggs, separated	*4 tbsp. butter or*
3½ cups milk	*margarine*
¼ cup flour	*2½ tsp. vanilla*
¼ tsp. salt	*Vanilla wafers*
1¾ cups sugar	*Bananas*

Beat egg yolks with milk and add to mixture of flour, salt, and 1½ cups sugar. Cook in a double boiler over medium heat until thickened. Remove from heat and stir in butter and vanilla. In the bottom of a loaf pan put a layer of vanilla wafers and then a layer of sliced bananas. Pour one half of the custard over them. Repeat. Whip egg whites until stiff, adding ¼ cup sugar near the end. Spoon meringue on top of pie and bake in 425° oven until meringue is slightly browned.

A generation ago in the Ozarks, where I farm, pies also served ro-
mance—and an unlikely adjunct, school finance—in what were known
as pie suppers. Back in those days of one-room schools in rural areas
with a poor tax base, pie suppers were an annual autumn event. Young
women would bake the best, the prettiest, the fanciest pies they could
and take them to the school in the evening for young men to bid on. The
top bidder would earn not only the pie but the right to eat it with its
baker. The money from the auction funded the school. The young
women would try to mark their pies in such a way that certain young
men would recognize them, and Ozark folklore is full of stories about
men who created emotional havoc by bidding—perhaps mistakenly,
perhaps not—on the "wrong" pie.

In addition to Pie Rules 1 and 2, there is another, which applies to the
entire country. Rule 3: Never eat pie within one mile of an interstate
highway. This rule eliminates pie in most fast-food restaurants and in
most truck stops, which are usually also franchises these days. I once
violated Rule 3 and had a disappointing piece of gooseberry pie at a
much recommended truck stop just off Interstate 70, between Kansas
City and St. Louis. But now I thought I had better check out the small,
independent truck stops, so I visited the Wyatt Junction Truck Stop, just
west of the Mississippi River, on U.S. 60. A sign on the wall said:

WELCOME TO

WYATT JUNCTION TRUCK STOP

TRUCKER'S NOTICE

ALL COFFEE FREE WITH

THE PURCHASE OF DIESEL FUEL

THANK YOU FOR COMING

HAVE

A

NICE

DAY

I ordered the dinner special: chicken-fried steak, fried bread, deep-fried okra, French-fried potatoes, and a tossed salad made almost entirely of fried bacon. A trucker in a black leather jacket came in looking enormously pleased and announced to no one in particular that he'd passed his sweetie about two hundred miles back and left her behind. He hoped she wasn't frosted. He put a quarter in the jukebox:

> The last thing I gave her was
> the bird,
> And she returned the favor with
> a few selected words. . . .
> Then left two streaks of Firestone
> smokin' on the street.

Sweetie pulled up and climbed out of her own eighteen-wheeler. She sauntered in. She had a fluffy shock of black hair and was wearing tight jeans, high-heeled red shoes, and a black leather jacket to match his. She glared at him and ordered Royal Crown Cola and apple pie. If she could, I could. I told the waitress to hold the R.C. but lemme have some pie. It was very like that served in the United States Senate Family Dining Room.

I was just a bit bilious by the time that I got to my farm, in southern Missouri, so I spent a couple of days there sucking on soda crackers and letting Tazzie visit her favorite places down by the river. I had heard about Opal Wheeler's Pie Factory, on U.S. 63, south of West Plains, but I'd never been there, and I enlisted the help of my friend Nancy for a pie foray. Nancy is a little bitty skinny woman who runs a health-food store and talks a lot about bean sprouts. She is always ready to try something new, however, and is a woman of considerable enthusiasm. We drove down U.S. 63 and found the Pie Factory, a cheery, small ten-sided building with white walls and red-trimmed windows. It would have been easy to miss, because it sits back from the road and has only a small, hand-painted sign to call attention to itself. Opal Wheeler is a grandmotherly-looking woman with a warm smile. She had been in the restaurant business for years before she and her sister drove by the newly constructed building in 1985. Her sister, who understood Opal's love of baking, pointed to it and said, "Opal, wouldn't that make a cute little pie factory?" Opal agreed, rented the place, put up the sign, and set to work. She starts rolling out pie dough on the counter in the center of the building each morning at about five-thirty. She is usually done baking by eleven, and the rest of the day she sells pies—sometimes whole, sometimes by the slice with coffee.

The day Nancy and I were there she had apple, apple-raisin, raisin, pecan, cherry, apricot, blueberry, pineapple-cream, peach-cream, cherry-cream, icebox mixed-fruit, strawberry-rhubarb, gooseberry, lemon-meringue, chocolate, coconut, banana, chocolate-delight (choco- late, pecans, cream cheese, single crust, whipped topping), lemon- delight, pecan-delight, and strawberry. I ordered a cup of coffee and told Nancy she could order whatever she wanted if she would talk to me about it. She began with a wedge each of apricot, apple-raisin, cherry, icebox mixed-fruit, and strawberry. And a cup of tea. "Oh, look," she said. "The crusts are sprinkled with sugar and browned. Pretty. . . . This apricot is too mooshy. . . . The apple-raisin is superior, though. I think it's the best one. . . . No, the cherry is the best—tart, lots of cherries, not much gooey filling. . . . No, maybe the mixed-fruit is my favorite. It's got a single crust, then a layer of cream cheese, then cherries with fresh pineapple. And this whipped topping! Wow! Can this lady make pies!"

"Anything else appeal to you?" I asked.

"Well, maybe I'll try a piece of lemon-meringue."

I watched in admiration as she ate that, too. Opal Wheeler freshened my coffee. I asked Nancy again which pie was best.

"How can I choose?" she asked. "Each one is a jewel."

"Nancy," I said, "you run a health-food store."

"Yeah, isn't it wonderful? She can make good pies out of stuff like this. I mean, white flour, white sugar, solid shortening? Maybe she could make the crusts out of whole-wheat flour. Oh, well, it just shows you what a talented cook can do."

Nancy left with an entire chocolate-delight pie in a box. She was happy, in perfect health, looking not one ounce fatter. And I was happy. I had always hoped that pies were good for us—a hope that had been encouraged by an article in the *Weekly World News* of October 27, 1987. I've long thought that there is a supermarket-tabloid headline designed to sucker every man, woman, or child at least once. Mine was SNICKERS AND TWINKIES MAKE YOU HEALTHY, SAYS FOOD EXPERT, touting an article declaring that there was "more nutrition in a Snickers bar or a Twinkie than in an apple." Might I not therefore assume, after watching Nancy tuck into her pies, that apple pie was the healthiest way to eat an apple?

In western Missouri, the good pie places thin out. The town cafés have become Daylight Donut outlets, to the detriment of both pies and doughnuts, but just at the border of Oklahoma I had an unexpectedly dainty and tasty chocolate pie at the Corners Minimart Motel & Café, on U.S. 60. The chocolate filling rested on a flavorful crust and was topped with a perfect, delicate meringue. Outside, prickly pear grew on the sunny south side of the restaurant, where there was a big white box with a sign on it that said:

CAUTION

BABY RATTLERS

Hints of the West.

Once I had crossed the Oklahoma line, I began seeing red-tailed hawks hunting high in the air above the road. It had been a long time since I'd heard a meadowlark sing. In one small town after another, waitresses in the cafés shook their heads when I asked for pie, and offered cobbler instead. "And mighty good cobbler it is, too," a customer informed me in the Hot Biscuit Café, in Vinita. But I drove on. There were sandburs at the rest stops, and Tazzie whimpered when she got them in her feet. The sun was warm. Spring had been in Oklahoma for some time. The sky opened up. I could see forever. The road threaded between hills covered with prairie grass, and someplace between Bartlesville and Ponca City I realized that I was in the West. I rolled down all the windows. *Ky-y-y-yr* screamed a red-tail overhead. I leaned out the window and the wind blew and tugged at my hair. *"Ky-y-yr,"* I screamed back. Fun. Can't do that on the interstate. The road was empty, and I was in love with driving. Out of nowhere, an Oklahoma trooper came up behind me and pulled me over. He reminded me that the speed limit was still fifty-five off the interstate, and gave me a "courtesy" ticket. Nice young man. Troopers know pie, so I asked him where he went to get it. He blushed a little, took off his hat, scratched his head, and thought awhile. Then, by way of explanation, he said, in his slow drawl, "Sorry, Ma'am, but you're in cobbler country now."

(March 1989)

T W O

Happy
New Year!

When I was growing up in Michigan my family never ate Hopping
John—black-eyed peas and rice—on New Year's Day for good
luck in the coming year. I don't know why. Perhaps we were too
far from the South, where some say the tradition started. Or perhaps we
were too dour a family to believe in good luck. It wasn't until I moved
to the Ozarks, years later, that I heard of the custom. Here, one New
Year's Day, the banker's wife telephoned me and asked me to dinner.
She is a splendid cook and I accepted happily. I was astonished to be
served a plateful of black-eyed peas and rice, plainer food than I'd ever
eaten at her table. She noticed my surprise, and laughed. "You don't
know about Hoppin' Johnny?" she asked. "Eating it on New Year's Day
is supposed to bring good luck in the coming year." She is a school-
teacher and was embarrassed to give credit to what sounded like a
hillbilly superstition. "Some say that you'll have as much money as the
peas you eat. Some cook up the rice with a piece of money in it, and the

person who gets the money in his serving will be rich. That's all non-sense of course, but it's fun to keep custom. People here have been doing it for generations."

On New Year's Days since then I have eaten Hopping John with greens in Arizona, Hopping John with ham in New York City, and I've fixed it myself in various ways and various places in between. And very fine years I've had afterward, thank you.

African-Americans claim the tradition is their own, a centerpiece of soul cookery, and point to the fact that it was their slave ancestors who introduced both black-eyed peas and rice to America. They cite the many ways cooks use black-eyed peas in Africa (one book lists sixty-some recipes), where cowpeas, the more usual name of *Vigna unguiculata*, were native. Some French-Canadians insist the tradition is theirs, add that there is a similar one in French-speaking Louisiana. To be sure, the association of the New Year with beans and good luck in France and elsewhere in Europe dates back to the Romans. And black-eyed peas are, of course, not peas (genus *Sativa*) at all, but beans (genus *Vigna*). Californian Japanese-Americans say they brought the custom with them to this country. And, yes, ancient Japanese tradition does call for the head of the house to go through his rooms on the stroke of midnight on the last day of the year carrying a box of cooked beans, which he scatters as he chants "Go forth demons! Enter riches!"

"Oh sure," said Stephanie Hall, folklorist at the American Folklife Center at the Library of Congress in Washington, D.C., when I asked her about Hopping John. "I know about it. Nobody seems to have studied it much; I can't find any papers on the subject. But I remember eating Hopping John on New Year's Day when I was growing up in North Carolina. We had black-eyed peas with collard greens, not rice as I understand some people do, because both represented money. The peas are copper colored. They are the change. The collard greens are folding money. I wouldn't tell this to the aunt who cooked the Hopping

John, but what we have here is sympathetic magic. Pork, in different forms, is sometimes added to it. Do you know about that?" she asked with a laugh. "You're supposed to eat pork on New Year's Day because a hog roots forward, and not chicken, which you eat at Christmas, because it scratches backward. There are a lot of New Year's Day eating customs like that. The Pennsylvania Dutch, for instance, eat sauerkraut and pork on New Year's Day. In other German households, cabbage and herring are consumed. You might want to take a look at Scottish New Year's Day customs, which involve the dark-eyed man who is supposed to come through the door on New Year's Day to bring good luck."

English, Scotch-Irish, and Highland Scots were some of the early white settlers in the Carolinas, states that claim Hopping John as their regional food, and they would have brought with them a variety of folk beliefs rooted in pre-Christian times. The Celtic New Year, earlier than the one we celebrate now, came on 1 November. It was a day when old scores were settled, the dead dismissed, the powers of witches and ghosts neutralized, and good fortune sought for the coming year. Fires were kindled, as they were to mark this and other of the year's festivals in many parts of the world. Bits of charred wood from these fires were pulled out and cherished for their potency—they were reputed to work cures and bring good fortune throughout the year. People danced around the fires and, as they burned down, leaped or hopped across them, perhaps to let the smoke drive out that which was bad or unfortunate in their lives. (Theodore Gaster, in his revision of James G. Frazer's *Golden Bough*, points out that part of the Muslim New Year celebrations that continued well into the twentieth century was to hop over fires crying, "We shake out upon thee, O bonfire, fleas and lice and sicknesses of heart and bones.") In northern England "hopping" is still a word for a wake, derived from the Anglo-Saxon *hoppan*, a religious dance or leap. Even after the present calendar was adopted, it continued to be important, in England and Scotland, to have a piece of charred wood in the house on New Year's Day, and it was (and still is in the Ozarks or other places where the belief endures) considered to be good luck to have a man with dark hair and dark eyes be the first to enter the house on New Year's Day, particularly if he is carrying a bit of charcoal, a piece of charred wood, or even a coal shovel.

Old calendars needed catch-up days to bring them into synchrony with the seasons. Many cultures considered those days, inserted at the end of one year and the beginning of the next, to be days outside of time, when the usual strictures need not apply, a time of festival and misrule. Presumably because it was so much fun, this custom continued even after the calendar was reformed. In northern Europe and England beans were associated with this rowdy time at the year's end and beginning, especially by the peasants and country folk. Black-eyed peas, native to warmer climates, might not have been known in the early days in northern Europe, but other beans were. In January, families elected a King and Queen of Bean, the commoners' Lords of Misrule: a special cake with a bean baked into it was served to the family, and the one to receive the bean in his slice was elected as ruler. Sir James Frazer wrote that the registers of Merton College, Oxford, record that the Fellows annually elected a Rex Fabarum (King of Bean) as Lord of Misrule, who held office until Candlemas Day, 2 February, to preside over revels, plays, and games for the students. I asked an old Mertonian about this, and he said that to this day the custom is remembered, if not practiced.

The English custom probably went back as far as the Roman occupation and the celebration of the feast of Saturnalia. In early Rome, the lemures and lares, ghosts and spirits of the family dead, were placated twice a year, in the summer and what was then the beginning of the new year, February. At those times the master of the family threw black beans over his head while chanting "I redeem myself and my family by these beans." An even older Greek invocation for protection against ghosts was to spit beans at them. I had been startled when my friend the banker's wife served me common black-eyed peas. But beans have always been a folk food: cheap, nutritious, well suited to elevate the householder to king, to turn each husband into his own exorcist. But beans, perhaps because they *are* common, were believed to contain the souls of the dead, according to Pliny in his *Historia Naturalis*. And so, for the rich and powerful, the priests of Rome and, even earlier, the priests of Egypt, beans were taboo. Here we arrive at the point where high spiritual rationalization meets low music-hall comedy and requires delicacy to explain. Let me turn the matter over to Robert Graves, poet and classicist, who writes in *The White Goddess:*

The Platonists excused their abstention from beans on the rationalistic ground that they caused flatulence; but this came to much the same thing [as the taboo against eating beans on the ground that one was eating souls]. Life was breath, and to break wind after eating beans was a proof that one had eaten a living soul—in Greek and Latin the same words, *anima* and *pneuma,* stand equally for gust of wind, breath, and soul or spirit.

Traditions in many cultures call for preventing anything from leaving the house on New Year's Day, insisting new things be brought into it instead. ("It ain't much trouble just for one day," an Ozarker told folklorist Vance Randolph as he insisted Randolph bring a stick of firewood into his shanty, "and me an' Maw don't aim to take no chances.") New Year's Day traditions also call for eating foods that begin small and swell as they cook. In parts of northern, beanless Europe, for instance, groats (fragments of dried wheat) were cooked to fluffiness and became a part of New Year's fare. How interesting, how fortuitous, how magical it must have seemed to the white Carolinian cooks to discover the black-eyed peas that their black slaves knew, a bean that came in many shades, ranging from copper to red, but always with its own pair of black eyes, which fitted in so well with their belief that a dark man with black eyes should be the first in their door on the year's first day.

By early in the eighteenth century, black people, sometimes coming from Africa via the Caribbean, made up the majority of the population in the Carolinas. And with them came their food. The African kings who had sold them into slavery also profited from selling food for the voyage and as an item of trade thereafter. In this way many foods from that continent—okra, palm oil, and a variety of beans, to name just a few— became part of African trade between the Old World and the New. Among the beans were cowpeas, the black-eyed peas. In Africa they have many names, depending upon the language spoken, including *kondi* (echoed, perhaps, in Louisiana Creole as *congri*), *agwa, soso, isanje, wake, yo,* or *adua,* but they are not called anything like "Hopping John." In Ghana, cooked with rice, they are called *yoo-ke-omo.* By the 1770s, at least, their cultivation was well established in America: Thomas Jefferson lists them in his 1774 *Garden Book,* noting that on 3 August "black eyed peas come to table."

Black-eyed peas, or other beans, are good nutritious food. And combining them with rice makes them even better, a matter discovered by regional cooks the world over, whether they knew the science behind the fact or not. The protein value of foods is related to the pattern of essential amino acids in them. Rice and beans, separately, both lack certain different amino acids, but when combined they complement and supplement those lacks and together provide a very high-quality protein, comparable to that of chicken or milk. Beans and rice keep body and soul together.

William H. Wiggins is author of *Freedom! Afro-American Emancipation Celebrations* and professor of Afro-American Studies and Folklore at Indiana University, Bloomington. "I am not aware," he told me, "of any association of good luck with black-eyed peas in African cultures, but it was the slaves who brought the ingredients of Hopping John to the Carolinas and also brought with them the knowledge of their cultivation. Many of the farms were small—they were sort of mom-and-pop affairs—and everyone on them, slave and slaveholder alike, lived together, went to church together, ate together. And I think that the custom of eating Hopping John at New Year's to bring luck and fortune is a good example of cultural sharing. The Africans brought the food and the Europeans brought the lore. Together they made a blended cultural tradition. Culture is conservative; it is the last thing to change. But it does change when people live together."

Where did that wonderful, slangy name "Hopping John" come from? In passing, it should be noted that red beans and rice are called Limping Susan (although some North Carolinians would substitute okra and bacon for the beans). And black beans and rice are Moors and Christians.

Explanations of the name are several, bizarre, ad hoc. One has it that children were required to hop around the table before eating black-eyed peas and rice. That sounds odd, unless we can believe that some residue of the Celtic fire hoppings made its way down the centuries. A local Ozark story says that a hungry guest named John was once invited to "hop in, John" and help himself. But the name has been around long before there were tellers of Ozark tales. One etymological explanation is that the name is a corruption of the French *pois à pigeon,* or No-Eye pea of Africa, common in the French-speaking Caribbean. *Pigeon* itself may be a corruption of a word that became the botanical name for this bean, *Catjanus cajan,* coming higgledy-piggledy through Malay, Dutch, and Boer as *katjang* or *kacang,* a word used for a variety of beans, including, confusingly, one subspecies of cowpea, *Vigna unguiculata cylindrica.* To be sure, when *pigeon* is pronounced the French way it sounds a bit like *John,* but this doesn't really work as an etymological explanation because the term "Hopping John" has its own crooked, straying history.

The first recipe I could find for a dish identified as Hopping John was dated 1847. It is in a book titled *The Carolina Housewife* and was written by Sarah Rutledge, hiding behind an authorial "Lady of Charleston."

HOPPING JOHN

One pound of bacon, one pint of red peas, one pint of rice. First put on the peas, and when half boiled, add the bacon. When the peas are well boiled, throw in the rice, which must be first washed and gravelled. When the rice has been boiling half an hour, take the pot off the fire and put it on coals to steam, as in boiling rice alone. Put a quart of water on the peas at first, and if it boils away too much, add a little more hot water. Season with salt and pepper, and, if liked, a sprig of green mint. In serving up, put the rice and peas first in the dish, and the bacon on the top.

In 1856, Frederick Law Olmsted, the American landscape architect, published a book titled *Journey in the Seaboard Slave States,* and in it he reported a conversation with a South Carolinian who criticized the character of young people in his home state. Sounding as the older generation always does in its observations of the younger, the man lamented "the descendents of the former proprietors of nearly all the land . . . have been brought up in a listless aimlessness and idle independence. . . . Their chief sustenance is a porridge of cow-peas and the greatest luxury with which they are acquainted is a stew of bacon and peas, with red pepper, which they call 'Hopping John.' "

But the disreputable commonness of such a dish had already been noted, albeit not quite as the same meal. In 1838, Caroline Gilman published her *Recollections of a Southern Matron* and referred to something called Hopping John that was made of bacon and rice, and added that it was "a good dish, to be sure, but no more presentable to strangers at the South than baked beans and pork in New England."

And in a raffish, puckish twist, surely a prank played by a Lord of Misrule or a King of Bean, the first printed reference to Hopping John comes from England. It is dated 1830, and occurs in George Cruikshank's *Three Courses and a Dessert.* Cruikshank mentions a beverage that sounds suspiciously like a poor man's wassail, the traditional festive drink frequently served at those festivals associated with the beginning and end of the year.

What d'ye say to Hopping John, made Tom Nottle's fashion? Landlord, mix a pint of brandy wi' half a gallon of your best cider, sugared to your own taste; and pop in about a dozen good roasted apples, hissing hot, to take the chill off.

Compare, please, to the American frontier tipple known as applejack, the brandy anyone could make when he let cider harden. To further stir up trouble, let the King of Bean point out that the usual basis for wassail, before the spices and apples are added, is ale, a "hopped" drink, to use a brewing term. It is made from an infusion of malt with hops added.

Our King of Bean has marched us around a corkscrew path, laughing at us from the shadows, I suspect.

The standard printed etymological and folklore sources say that the origin of the term "Hopping John" is unknown.

"I don't know," said Folklorist Hall, when I asked her about the term.

"I don't know," Professor Wiggins echoed. But William Wiggins does have his own favorite recipe for Hopping John, which his wife, Janice, has prepared every New Year's Day for almost thirty years. Here it is. Perhaps you'd like to try it. And good luck. Happy New Year!

HOPPING JOHN

BLACK-EYED PEAS

2 smoked ham hocks	*Bay leaf*
1-lb. package	*Cayenne pepper*
black-eyed peas,	*Black pepper*
thoroughly rinsed	*Garlic powder*
and drained	*Cajun spice*
Salt	

Place the ham hocks in a pot containing about 3 inches of cold water. Cover and place over very high heat. Once the water comes to a boil, add the rinsed black-eyed peas. Lower heat, and add seasonings. Cover pot and cook until done, stirring occasionally and adding small amounts of cold water as needed.

STEAMED RICE

*2 cups white rice,   Cold water to cover
thoroughly rinsed
and drained*

Place rinsed rice in pot, add cold water. Cover pot and heat over high flame. When steam appears, remove pot from heat and let rice steam, covered, until done. Serve with a large onion, chopped; hot sauce; and fresh cornbread. Serves 6 to 8.

(December 1993)

Hey, Presto!

*Contiguity and succession are not sufficient to make
us pronounce any two objects to be cause and effect.*

—David Hume,
A Treatise of Human Nature *(1739–40)*

*Magic is a mind-expanding art form because it
demonstrates that the boundaries of perception
aren't necessarily the boundaries of reality.*

—*Jay Scott Berry, California magician, at the 53rd Annual
Magic Get-Together, Colon, Michigan, 1990*

Colon, Michigan, is the magic capital of the world. You know that's
true because the sign at the village limits says so:

WELCOME TO

COLON

MAGIC CAPITAL OF

THE WORLD

1832 SESQUICENTENNIAL 1982

1989 CLASS D

STATE BASEBALL CHAMPIONS

Colon is a village of eleven hundred people in southwestern Michigan, in flat prairie farmland. It is a village of two-story Victorian houses
and smaller, modest ones, each nestled into an ample, well-tended yard,
and there are gardens big enough to grow sweet corn two blocks from

the intersection of the two main roads, State Street and Blackstone Avenue. The avenue is named for Colon's most famous past resident, Harry Blackstone, the magician: Blackstone the Great, né Henry Boughton, who came there in 1926, and for whom it was home, as much as any place could be for a traveling entertainer. It has more parks than anything else, and maple trees—big, overarching ones—really do grow on Maple Street. And there is not a place in the village where you can't hear the cooing of mourning doves on a summer day.

Colon is also the home of Abbott's Magic Manufacturing Company, founded by Percy Abbott, an Australian magician, in 1934, a few years after a Blackstone–Abbott magic company, started in 1927, failed, and Blackstone and Abbott had a falling out. With a million dollars in annual sales, made mostly through a three-pound mail-order catalog, Abbott's is the biggest magic manufacturer in the world, according to the present owner, Greg Bordner. And for a time in late summer of each year since the 1930s there have been more magicians around Colon than anywhere else on earth. The occasion is the Magic Get-Together, cosponsored by Abbott's and the Colon Lions. Magicians are a clubby lot and hold other meetings, but those are usually in big cities. According to Harry Blackstone, Jr., a magician in his own right, the Get-Together is the meeting that all magicians look forward to, because of the rural setting and the air of sociability. A thousand magicians, perhaps a few more—some full-time performers, the rest part-timers and amateurs—come to Colon from around the world, and take over the village. For twenty years now, Blackstone himself has been coming back to his hometown (he went to school here for a year or two, and still owns a bit of land on what is called Blackstone Island, in Sturgeon Lake).

I grew up in Kalamazoo, about twenty-five miles to the northwest as the crow flies. I was the easiest kid in the world to fool; for a while, I cherished the notion that I had a head full of nickels, because my father could produce them so easily from my ears. In those days, I was a pushover for the public performances held in Colon in the evenings during the Get-Togethers. I can remember the aura of those evening shows, shows that I attended forty years ago and more: the dark stage, the bright colors, flowers, floating scarves, capes in black and red, and the daring, slightly wicked quality of dying vaudeville.

This past August, I decided to pay a nostalgic visit to Colon to see what happens when a thousand magicians come to town. It was the 53rd Annual Magic Get-Together. Colon may be only twenty-five miles from Kalamazoo, but in order to get there I had to take out a map and look up which turns to take on state and county roads—a process lending substance to a conceit that Bordner and Blackstone like to maintain in interviews, that Colon is like Brigadoon, a hard-to-find place that disappears except during Get-Together time. I had known Harry Blackstone when we were both eighteen, and, seeing him recently in California, where he lives, I had asked him what growing up in Colon was like. "Shades of gray," he said, with a sigh. I knew what he meant. When I was growing up, I was under the impression that the sun vanished in October and was not seen again by humankind until May. The weather, blowing in from Lake Michigan, was bleak, cold, damp, and dark for much of the year.

On the first day of the 53rd Get-Together, however, Michigan was at its winsome best. It was a clear, sunny, high-pressure day, with blue skies and fluffy white clouds, and the corn was greening in the fields. In the village, I parked under a shady tree, because Tazzie, my dog, was with me. I walked over to the Abbott plant, a low cement-block building that would look like a radiator-repair shop if it were not painted black with white skeletons dancing across its front. I passed a knot of people on the street. "How d'ya like this?" a man was asking. He shook his wrist, and bright-red carnations bloomed from his fingertips. The members of his tiny audience nodded, smiled, and applauded. Inside the Abbott office I picked up my registration papers. I've never quite recovered from being fooled about those nickels, so I had paid the full professional fee, seventy-five dollars, to be allowed to attend not only the four public evening shows but also the dealers' showrooms and the workshops, lectures, and demonstrations. In my envelope of materials I found a plastic badge with my name on it and a cord attached, and I hung it around my neck to separate myself from the ordinary citizens of Colon. I peered inside the Abbott showroom. It was a dark room with creaky wooden floors, and its walls and ceiling were covered with magicians' posters, including one of the senior Blackstone, backlit to emphasize his aureole of white hair. The room was lined with glass cases that looked like old-fashioned candy-display counters but were filled with magic tricks, and in the center of the room an Abbott employee was putting on a magic show, mostly for children.

It was only ten in the morning, but magicians were already arriving in town, many of them in vans and oversized campers. Colon has no hotels, no motels, no inns. Some of the magicians camp out in the parks, but more rent rooms or houses from the residents. And many pairings of guest and landlord have stayed the same over the years, giving the Get-Together a mixed quality, of friendship and cash crop. Yard sales were springing up all over town, and I talked to the proprietor of one. She told me she was renting out a room to a magician couple who had been staying with her each August for the past ten years. "When my husband was alive, we used to rent out nearly every room in the house, and all our outbuildings, too," she said. "Haven't done that since he's been gone. But I've been thinking about all the campers that come these days. I guess I'll get me a batch of Porta Pottis next year and set them up and rent out the yard."

I walked up State Street, where all the merchants had stenciled signs in their windows that said WELCOME MAGICIANS alongside posters for a circus that was coming to nearby Three Rivers later in the month, and out along the creek, past the dam that makes Palmer Lake. Beyond the dam I found the elementary school, where many of the activities were to take place. Just inside the school door, a uniformed security guard with a big smile was checking every plastic badge. The school gym and a couple of classrooms were filled to overflowing with magic wares and books, in odd contrast to the little desks and sober blackboards, and magicians were busily taking over rooms for workshops, demonstrations, and sales booths.

The magicians—most of whom were men—talked magic, passed out business cards, did magic, passed out business cards, bought magic, passed out business cards, demonstrated gimmicks, passed out business cards. "Gimmick" is a magicians' word that has entered everyday language. It refers to that device or object—that invisible wire, false fingertip, hidden lever—which makes the magic possible. Magicians use other words specially. Scarves are called "silks." "Disappear" and "vanish" are transitive verbs, as in "I vanished the ball" and "He disappeared the girl." "Tricks" are small pieces of magic—the silk that turns into a dove, the cut and knotted rope that mends itself. "Illusions" are big pieces of magic. Illusions are pricey; they can cost many thousands of dollars. Abbott's has made many of them over the years, some to order: Houdini's underwater torture box; Blackstone's buzz saw; David Copperfield's straitjacket; the device that disappeared an elephant, for which Abbott's furnished everything except the elephant. One whole wall of the gym was covered with a display of books: *How to Sell by Magic, Nite Club Illusions, Conjurors' Psychological Secrets,* and so on. Heaped on shelves along another wall were Abbott's offerings: Dove Through the Glass ($135), Elusive Bunny Box ($100), Mirror Tumbler ($5), Disecto ($90), and more objects in Day-Glo colors and shiny metal than I could take in.

Greg Bordner was standing near the Disecto, expansive, cheerful, busy. A handsome, athletic-looking man in his late thirties, he is a political-science graduate of Michigan State, and the son of Recil Bordner, a magician who was Percy Abbott's partner after Abbott broke with

Blackstone. Versions of the cause of the split vary, but all agree that the two men, both strong-willed, clashed over the financial end of the business, and that Blackstone, the bigger of the two, came over to Abbott's house one night, beat him up, and stalked out. According to Bordner, Abbott called the police, and when they arrived Blackstone walked back in and greeted Abbott like an old friend—"Hi, Percy, it's been a while. Good to see you"—thus flummoxing the police. But, Bordner said, Blackstone stayed so angry that whenever he saw Abbott in the grocery store he would pull canned goods off the shelves and hurl them at him. He also tried to start a rival magic show and manufacturing company, and refused to perform for the Abbott Get-Together until 1961, when he was seventy-five. Though his skills were failing, he came from California to perform in a sentimental return; when he died, in 1965, his ashes were buried in the cemetery at Colon, where they lie under a stone that appears to be part flower, part flame. According to Bordner, more magicians—around a dozen—are buried in that cemetery, along with Blackstone, than anywhere else in the world.

I asked Bordner about the Disecto, and, confiding that he was only a fourth-rate magician, he got it out. It looks like a simple wooden stand with a big hole in the center and two little holes above and below. At the top is a sharp-looking knife that raises and lowers like a cleaver. The cleaver slices through carrots placed in the little holes. Bordner put his arm in the big hole and dropped the cleaver. His hand was just fine when he pulled it out. I gasped. I couldn't help myself. "How did you do that?"

Bordner grinned and said, "The trick's told when the trick's sold." He invited me on a tour of his empire, and we went back to the Abbott building. Behind the display room was a dark, Dickensian stockroom lined with drawers bearing labels like RABBIT WRINGER and FLOWER SURPRISE. There orders were being filled for Sweden and Japan. We walked past a set of sinks where silks are dyed and the staff makes coffee, then went downstairs to a room where a woman was making magical silk flowers, stitching away and listening to country music on the radio. Outside again, Bordner put a big box of outgoing mail in the back seat of his Chevy ("The magic business isn't what it used to be. My father drove a Buick") and drove me over to the workshop, a nondescript blue-and-white metal building on the edge of town, next to the supermarket. Except for a preponderance of rabbits, it looked like an ordinary wood-and-metal shop. Tacked to the walls were snapshots of magician customers, including one of a Nigerian prince who once came, with an entourage, to the Get-Together. He placed a big order for illusions and had them shipped home. Bordner shook his head over the prince. "He billed himself as someone who had Powers," he said. Bordner doesn't approve of Powers; he doesn't like to associate magic with the paranormal. He made a face. "Hey, this is just a business. We manufacture tricks and illusions. I know the U.P.S. rates anywhere."

I very much wanted to buy a trick. Back at the elementary school, I asked around about the gimmick used for one of the world's oldest recorded magic tricks. In the Bible, in Exodus, we are told how Aaron so impressed Pharaoh with wonders and magic that Pharaoh let the people of Israel leave Egypt. Aaron showed Pharaoh a rod and changed it into a snake. Pharaoh called his magicians, and they also turned rods into snakes, but then Aaron caused his snake to eat up theirs. Bordner laughed when I asked him about it, and said he didn't have a trick like that. "Maybe one of the snake handlers could help you," he added. He looked around the gym-salesroom, but couldn't spot a snake handler at the moment. I moved on to another salesman, who was doing impossible things with what looked like a solid hoop of gleaming metal. It became a square, then a flat strip. "Oh, yeah, I know that trick," he said when I asked. "I got a wand that turns into a snake, but it's not a very good snake. I mean, it isn't a python or a cobra, or anything." I watched a New Age magician, Jay Scott Berry, who was dressed in black and had long, curly blond hair, produce a brilliant flash of light from his fingertip:

"Uses no batteries." Then he transformed a rainbow-colored bar into gold.

"Ummm!" said a watching magician. "That's smooth."

"Ye-ahh," said Berry, changing from entertainer into salesman. "I worked a long time to get it so smooth." He was monopolizing the crowd, to the chagrin of a Japanese magician at the next booth, who smiled bravely as he plucked fire from the air and lit a fire in the palm of first one hand, then the other.

I settled for a trick called the Amazing Keybender ("Yes, you can bend keys and spoons"), which I bought from Abbott's for five dollars. It is a small, simple gimmick, and comes with three pages of directions which include the plea "All we ask is that you do not claim to have supernatural powers," and add archly, "One doing that is enough"—a prim reference to Uri Geller. I practiced the trick at home after the Get-Together, but no one applauded. "What do you have up your sleeve?" my stepson asked at my first and only family performance. That brings me to the basic secret of magic: the gimmicks are simple, but the tricks are hard, and require impressive skills and dexterity, and a keen sense of psychology for misdirecting the audience's attention. Every evening during the Get-Together, there was a public show, and during the day spontaneous shows never stopped: a thousand magicians showing off to a thousand magicians, receiving and giving applause and appreciation. They all knew the gimmicks. What they were applauding was the skill in their use, the quick hands and sly diversions, the breaking apart of cause and effect, forcing the senses to trick the brain.

Colon grows weirder and weirder. Everywhere magicians' vans are parked. Magicians nap in folding chairs. Magicians sell magic to one another. Magicians sit on curbs and throw their voices, so that trash cans begin to twitter like birds. At the counter of the M & M Grill, a stocky man in glasses hits his hand on the counter—*whack! whack!*—disappearing fuzzy balls every time. His companion nods appreciatively while he eats his cheeseburger. There would be applause from the booth behind them, except that one of the six magicians sitting there has the attention of the rest, asking them to pick a card from the fan of cards he holds in his hand. Jugglers fill the parks. I talk to a young juggler named Steve. "I do magic, too, but I prefer juggling," he says. "There are lots of jugglers around these days, because we had parents who were hippies who took up juggling; it was supposed to represent psychic balance, or something. We don't go in for that stuff, but we learned how to juggle from them. I'd like to get a job on a cruise ship or work in a theme park." Theme-park magicians, I learn at an afternoon workshop, are paid seven hundred dollars a week, and must do five shows a day, six days a week. Cruise ships pay from four hundred dollars a week to eighteen hundred; the occupational hazard is weight gain from good food.

Waiting for the evening performance, in the high-school auditorium, I take Tazzie out for a romp in the meadow behind the high school. She leaps from the car and begins running joyous circles around a young, sinister-looking man with punked hair dyed flat black, who is wearing black pants, slightly pegged, and a black shirt—the preferred dress of young magicians. With him is a savage-looking girl with purple makeup and a mane of black hair, who is wearing a black leather miniskirt. They squat down and scratch Tazzie on the belly, transforming themselves into teenagers. A clown is working out on a unicycle in the school-bus parking lot. Tazzie finds gopher holes to dig out, and I lie down in the clover, listening to the doves and the katydids. Overhead, swallows circle and swoop. How do they do that?

Later, inside the auditorium, women in sequinned gowns float in the air. One, to the amusement of the audience, refuses to be sawed in two and forces the magician to take her place inside the specially designed box. Ropes cut and heal themselves, and knots in them slide and disappear. Needles are stuck into balloons without popping them. Coins multiply. Cards are chosen and told. Silks appear from nowhere. A thousand magicians and six or seven hundred other spectators cheer and applaud under a banner celebrating the Class D Baseball Championship. (The team is called the Magi; its mascot is a white rabbit coming out of a hat.) The seats are hard and cramped, the sound system crackles and occasionally fails, but the performances are slick, smooth, very Big Time, paced for television. Last year's young-talent-contest winner has been invited back for a segment of an evening show: he presents a display of leggy girls, dancing, and other flourishes that looks as though he had MTV in mind. Other magicians use backdrops with their names in flashing lights and work to a rock-and-roll beat. Blackstone's segment is filmed for a TV show to be broadcast next spring. Magicians from Switzerland and Czechoslovakia are featured, calmer and wittier than the Americans, who are from a vaudeville tradition. A contingent of Indians comes into the auditorium, the women dressed in saris. I ask a gray-haired matron with an empty seat beside her if it is taken. "It's my husband," she says. "I vanished him."

One morning, I dropped in on the Vent-O-Rama. Ventriloquists call themselves "vents," and the Vent-O-Rama is a workshop for them. Ventriloquism has long been a part of the Get-Together. Edgar Bergen was born in nearby Dowagiac, and sometimes attended the Get-Together with Charlie McCarthy and Mortimer Snerd. "The *Pythonists* spake hollowe; as in the bottome of their bellies, whereby they are aptlie in Latine called *Ventriloqui*," Reginald Scot wrote, in 1584, in *The Discoverie of Witchcraft*, which is said to be the oldest surviving text on magic tricks. Not only does Scot discuss ventriloquism; he says that if one is not a "sluggard," a "niggard," or a "dizzard" one can learn to perform "Magicke," and proceeds to give detailed directions. While reading that 400-year-old handbook, I was pleased to note that my father had been no dizzard: his nickel-from-the-ear trick is detailed by Scot under the heading "Of conveiance of monie." It is done by "palming," the word that magicians use to describe the way to hold a coin, card, or other small object hidden between the fingers or on the back or front of an apparently empty hand. You and I don't have muscles trained to do that, but they do. ("This is hard," said Doug Anderson at an afternoon workshop, as he demonstrated how to make a coin appear to jump straight up from his motionless hand. "It was painful to learn how to squeeze my palm muscles. Broke some blood vessels, too.")

Scot's may be the oldest handbook of magic tricks, but conjuring, or trickster magic, has an even older history. Aaron and the Egyptian magicians with their wand-snakes were not the only ones in antiquity to use gimmicks. (Aaron's most famous trick, making a rod bloom with flowers—by which he established the preeminence of the tribe of his brother, Moses, over the eleven other tribes of Israel—can be found in the Abbott mail-order catalog: the Flower Wand, under "Flowers that bloom WITH a spring, tra la!," for four dollars.) What is thought to be the first self-moving vehicle was designed by Hero of Alexandria, an engineer who flourished around the beginning of the first millennium. It was used to make gods and goddesses move upon their altars, revolve, and produce milk and wine as if by miracle. Egypt, Greece, Persia, Rome, China, and India all had magicians, and some of their tricks—Cups and Balls and the Hindu Rope Trick, to name two—are part of modern magicians' stock-in-trade.

The morning I was at the Vent-O-Rama, the principal vent had a cold and a sore throat, so he asked the vents perched on tables and chairs around the classroom to volunteer. Almost before the words were out of his mouth, a young woman with red hair called out "Me . . . me . . . me!" and ran to the front of the room with two oversized stuffed toys. (Magicians are not shy. Boffo routine in the evening show: the MC says, "Tonight, we have the world's greatest magician with us. Will he stand up, please?" A thousand magicians leap to their feet, and everyone applauds.) I watched the red-haired ventriloquist as her stuffed toys carried on a lunatic conversation with her. Her mouth didn't move; her throat muscles didn't even quiver. How does she do it? When she returned to her seat, amid applause, to give way to the next performer, she regained our attention momentarily, and received some appreciative chuckles, by throwing her voice to the front of the room.

In the village, the good people of Colon were busily turning goods and services into dollar bills. In the general store, a troupe of young magicians was buying cotton balls. "Gonna have a new opening to-night," one of the women said. And, sure enough, that evening I saw those mundane cotton balls deftly appear and disappear between out-stretched fingers.

I talked to Bob Kolb, the owner of Magic City Hardware, who is active in the Chamber of Commerce.

"You bet the Get-Together is good for the economy," he told me. "People rent out their houses. Some people even leave town for vacation and turn their houses over to the magicians. There are some real little houses here, and I've seen maybe ten magicians in a single one of them. Then, there are the fund-raisers. The Lutherans put on a big lunch, and the magicians like it, because they don't charge big-city prices. I sell the magicians nuts and bolts to fix their campers, and some big-ticket items, too. And then there are the merchants' sidewalk sales—how am I going to put this? We all have some stock. . . . Now, it isn't bad merchandise, it's just that folks in Colon haven't bought it all year. These magicians come from all over—California, New York, Canada—and their tastes are, um, different, so we sell it to them. We unload a lot of stuff that way."

Craft sales began to appear among the yard sales. Soon it seemed that every third house had something for sale: wrought-iron trivets, odd dinner plates, hand-painted ceramics, little wooden benches, children's outgrown clothes, plastic purses. Curbside-parked cars had FOR SALE signs in their windows. Amish had driven in from farms in their buggies and were racing around town to snap up the best bargains before the magicians could get to them.

Having attended the Vent-O-Rama, I had missed the magicians' buffet lunch at the Lutheran church, a handsome new, sprawling building on the outskirts of the village, right next to the Enchanted Glen Apartments. Instead, I went over to the Grange Hall, on Blackstone Avenue, for the Pig Roast. Inside the hall were long tables covered with oilcloth. A motherly-looking woman served me barbecue, baked beans, two homemade molasses cookies, and a cup of iced tea, for three dollars and ten cents. This was a fund-raiser. It was the first time the Grange had put one on, she told me. "Some years back, the Lutherans used to serve dinner every evening during the Get-Together. That's the way they raised the money to build the church." The church that magic built.

After a whole day of magic and a three-hour evening performance, the magicians, their attention sharpened, tingling from their own applause, are high on magic, and reluctant to end the day. When the tourists (some three thousand of them paid to see the public shows during the week) have driven away, the magicians return to the Abbott showrooms for auctions of magic equipment, or they go over to the American Legion Hall, on State Street. I drop in at the hall about midnight. It is stuffed with magicians drinking beer, eating fries, laughing, and showing off. A T-shirted magician moves from table to table performing what I have learned to call closeup magic. He is applauded as he moves a safety pin from one corner of a square of red flannel to another without unpinning it. I find a place at a table with a group recalling their days on the road.

"D'you remember the night at the motel when we took the ice out of the ice machine and stuffed Ed inside?"

"Yeah. Remember the look on the face of that little old lady when she opened the machine door and he handed her a bucketful of ice?"

"Hey, how about the time in the hotel in Kentucky when we took the furniture out of our room and put it in the elevator, so that it looked like a sitting room, and rode up and down in it reading newspapers and watching the faces of the guests when the door opened for them?"

"Where was it that we filled up the motel swimming pool with Knox gelatin?"

The laughter grows louder; the air is thick with cigarette smoke, magic, and fellowship. At 2:00 A.M., the American Legion will close its doors and force the magicians out onto the street. They tell me about the young Doug Henning, seventeen or eighteen years old and unknown, who wandered around town one night after the hall closed until he found a twenty-four-hour Laundromat, the only public building with lights still on, and did magic tricks for his friends until dawn. His later fame has assured that it will forever be known as the Doug Henning Laundromat. Some years ago, they tell me, there was still enough of a crowd on the streets at 3:00 A.M. to respond to the request "Pick a card any card." And, just as someone in the small audience did so, and looked expectantly at the magician to identify it, a heavyset man lurched toward the spectators, stumbled on the curb, and fell. Several men reached out to help him up, and as he regained his feet his pants slithered to his ankles to reveal baggy undershorts with the card printed large upon them.

As the week progresses, there is far more magic on and off the streets of Colon than I can take in. The wild mourning doves are reproduced onstage in the white doves that flutter from silks, flowers, hats. A man balances a hundred and thirty-five cigar boxes on the end of his chin. Wands shoot confetti, and it settles in our hair. White bunnies are everywhere. Street musicians play. A lank-haired man in a polo shirt walks down State Street tossing up balls, and they vanish high in the air. "Hey, I like it. I like it," his companion says, slapping his knee. One evening, Harry Blackstone recreates one of his father's most famous performances. Taking a lighted lamp, with a stagily long electric cord, offered to him by his assistant—his wife, Gay—he removes the bulb. On the dim stage, the bulb remains shining eerily in his hand. He then apparently releases it, and it hovers dreamily about him in the darkness.

He sends it, glowing, down to the front rows of the audience, where he invites spectators to touch it and reassure themselves of its substance. When a doubter farther back in the auditorium calls out, Blackstone says, with a smile, that he will send the bulb out to him. Luminous, spectral, the bulb—a mere light bulb, made lovely and strange by behaving in a way that no mundane light bulb should—drifts gently out over the audience and then soars back to its master, who returns it to the lamp. And I understand that I have never really seen a light bulb before.

One hot afternoon, I take Tazzie down past the dam to a little creek that runs from it. Tazzie wades into the water while I sit on the grassy bank and watch a pair of tiger swallowtails circle in the air above me. A pretty little girl with curly chestnut-colored hair comes walking down the bank from one of the houses nearby. "What's your dog's name?" she asks.

"Tazzie. What's your name?"

"Jessie. You know what?"

"What?"

"I'm four years old. Can Tazzie do tricks?"

"Not really. She likes to take rocks out of the water, though." I point to Tazzie, hard at work loosening from the bottom of the stream a rock much too big for her.

"Well, I can do a trick."

"You can?"

"Yes. I can put my head under water." And—hey, presto!—she does. Carefully pinching her nostrils, Jessie puts at least half an inch of her face into the water and very quickly pulls it out. She looks at me, expectant, proud. I applaud.

(November 1990)

F O U R

Space Aliens Take Over the U.S. Senate!!!

I am standing in one of the most unusual places I have ever been. It is an alcove in the big newsroom of the *National Enquirer*, Lantana, Florida. The newsroom is deep inside a one-story, pebbled concrete building with huge windows that make it look like an overgrown elementary school. The building is hidden by trees and lush tropical plants, surrounded by parking lot. Across the street is the neighborhood baseball diamond, and all around are modest, slightly seedy tract houses in pastel stucco with weedy yards. The crowded alcove where I am standing is jammed with the desks, computers, and files of the nineteen staffers who turn out the *Weekly World News,* the black-and-white supermarket tabloid that has taken newspapering to its absurdist, postpostmodern limits, the paper that screams from the rack at the checkout: WORLD WAR II BOMBER FOUND ON MOON. ELVIS IS ALIVE. FARMER SHOOTS 23 LB. GRASSHOPPER.

Eddie Clontz, its editor, sandy haired, smiley, bouncy, has invited me to spend the day in this alcove. His desk is heaped with green folders that contain the clips from hundreds of newspapers around the world, letters from readers, transcripts of telephone calls that are the "kernels" of *WWN* stories. The folders will be passed to the reporters who will embellish them and translate them into tabloidese (heroes are "spunky," children are "heartbreak tots," women are "gutsy moms," unusual sexual behavior is "sicko"). On top of the stack of folders is a rubber dog mask.

"Eddie," I say, "I can't help but notice you have a dog mask on your desk."

"Yeah. I wear it from time to time, but this is my real reporter-waker-upper," he says gleefully, as he opens his desk drawer and pulls out the biggest squirt gun I've ever seen. He aims it at Susan Jimison, B. A. University of Pennsylvania, specialist on Elvis sightings and people who have been held captive in alien space ships. She is staring meditatively out the window. "Susan!" he calls to her.

She looks up and groans theatrically, "Oh, no! Not again!" but Jack Alexander, Indiana University graduate, former bureau chief of the *St. Petersburg Times*, who has recently helped break the "story of the century"—that five U.S. senators are actually space aliens—chivalrously holds up his word-processor keyboard to block the shot.

Eddie laughs uproariously. "The expense of the electronics around here has never stopped me from using water on them."

His staff, unlike some of those on the other tabloids, where many are Brits, is American and stuffed with degrees from Harvard, Bryn Mawr, and other good schools. They include a veteran of *The New York Times*, a former Capitol Hill reporter for Newhouse News Service, the retired juvenile nonfiction editor for J. B. Lippincott. Salaries for established reporters are $75,000 and more. A recent hire, with no tabloid experience, has started at $53,000, and editors make salaries well into the comfortable six figures. In an unguarded moment, Eddie, himself a tenth-grade dropout, but former wire editor at the *St. Petersburg Times*, once confessed "We have to pay them a lot because we are, in effect, asking them to end their careers.... We are the French Foreign Legion of journalism."

It wasn't until after the death in 1988 of Generoso Pope, Jr., the father of the supermarket tabloid, that visitors have been allowed into this building. I feel privileged, at the heart of mystery. I turn to Sal Ivone, M. A. University of Chicago, former corporate speechwriter, managing editor of *WWN*. He is a thin, intense, dark-haired, mournful-eyed straight man to Eddie, the ebullient comedian. I ask him if I can meet the alien who, during the autumn of 1992, amused us at the supermarket checkout line by endorsing first George Bush, switching to Ross Perot, and finally settling on Bill Clinton. "Yeah, we might be able to arrange it," he says thoughtfully.

While waiting, I ask Eddie to tell me about "the story of the century," the discovery that space aliens are taking over the Senate. A principle of tabloid journalism from Fleet Street to Lantana states: Never question yourself out of a good story. Eddie explains:

We once had a couple of sisters call who had a ride in a UFO and unfortunately I gave it to a former daily newspaper reporter who asked if they'd ever been under psychiatric care. I had to let him go and I told him, "These are nice people and who are we to say they didn't go for a ride on a UFO? We aren't *The New England Journal of Medicine*, for Chris' sake." Well, we'd run the story about the alien endorsing the candidates and we got a call from a reader and he says "That guy, he's not the only alien around. I can't give you my name and don't try to trace this call, but John Glenn is a space alien . . . and . . . and . . . there are MORE!" I said "What the hell! Call 'em up. Maybe the whole damn Senate's made up of aliens."

Reporters started calling Senate offices. Many aides responded with incredulity; some hung up. But some didn't. Five senators, Glenn, Hatch, Kassebaum, Nunn, and Simpson, were under suspicion and two had aides with wit enough to admit the shocking truth. Said Glenn's spokesman, "Okay. Okay. You found us out, but remember this: man-kind is not alone." Nunn's aide responded, "I'm almost positive there are more," corroboration enough for a *WWN* story. The story, complete with pictures of all five senators and the capitol, was published. Nunn himself wrote to Eddie and it is my own journalistic scoop to reproduce his letter below.

What is this? Fiendishly clever political satire? Sal denies it, but there

---

SAM NUNN
GEORGIA

United States Senate
WASHINGTON, DC 20510-1001

January 13, 1993

Dear Eddie:

Thank you for the framed copies of the "Story of the Century" issue where you blew my cover. While I have not been asked to appear on "Deep Space Nine" your story about me being a space alien did generate a significant number of inquiries to my press office. I, of course, answered all the queries telepathically.

I appreciate the good humor of your staff; and thank you again for the memento of the story. It now hangs proudly in the reception area of my Senate office along with my collection of political cartoons.

May the force be with you.

Sincerely,

Sam Nunn

Eddie Clontz
Editor
Weekly World News
600 South East Coast Avenue
Lantana, Florida 33462

is a certain brightness in his eyes when I mention that such a piece reminded me of the satires I have heard on National Public Radio. Sal is, he confesses, a fan of *All Things Considered*. But Derek Clontz, a bearded, dryly witty man, assistant managing editor (and Eddie's brother), admits, "We write our stories in a flat, reportorial style, the way AP would. By virtue of doing that, those things begin to operate on two levels."

"When am I going to meet the alien?" I nag Sal.

"Y'know we don't let *tourists* in here unless it's real safe. We've got the landing pad for him out there in the parking lot. Hmmmm. Looks like it's pretty full of cars just now," Sal answers, peering out of the window through the tropical foliage.

Do readers believe what they read in the supermarket tabloids? Attitude surveys, for obvious reasons, are hard to conduct, but a Roper poll, taken in 1984, found 20 percent of respondents said the supermarket tabloids were "accurate," and 49 percent said they were not. Lest journalists from the straight press feel smug, I hasten to point out that another slightly different but comparable Roper poll, conducted the same year about the credibility of media in presenting conflicting reports, found that 24 percent trusted newspapers and only 7 percent trusted magazines.

Eddie likes to point out that he has 200 million readers every week. That is an estimate of how many people pass through the supermarkets and scan his cover while in the checkout line. Other, slightly calmer, sources claim that combined readership of the six national tabloids, with their assorted emphases on celebrity gossip, health, horoscopes, and the bizarre, is 50 million a week, based on sales here and abroad, plus the numbers of readers to whom purchased copies are passed on. But both estimates are "tabloid truth"—numbers with a kernel of reality. Audit Bureau of Circulation figures for U.S. weekly sales over the last half of 1991 (the most recent comparative statistics available) total a little under

11 million for all six, arranged in order of sales: *National Enquirer, Star, Globe, National Examiner, Weekly World News, Sun.* If each issue sold is passed on to a couple of other people, total readership may be somewhere between 25 to 30 million each week. Even without tabloid truth, that is a lot of readers, and, exempting pass-on readers, *National Enquirer, Star, Globe,* and *National Examiner* are among the top 100 best-selling U.S. magazines.

The usual assumption is that the average tabloid reader is a middle-aged woman who watches a lot of daytime television. However, no in-depth surveys have been done, and Sal and Eddie tell me that *WWN* is beginning to develop a cult readership among intellectuals. "We've got some college fan clubs," Eddie says, as Sal drapes me in *WWN* T-shirts featuring the front page of their biggest seller of all time: ELVIS IS ALIVE. *WWN* no longer tops the million mark in sales each week as it did back in the mid- to late-1980s, the glory days of all the tabloids, but it still runs comfortably ahead of its imitator in the Globe stable of tabloids, the *Sun,* which today sells under 500,000 copies each week.

The Globe publications, *Globe, National Examiner,* and *Sun,* have always trailed the others. "Pope led the way," Phil Bunton, corporate editor of Globe Communications, had told me. "We've just followed his lead." Globe Communications offices are showier than those of the *Enquirer.* They are in nearby Boca Raton, in the area dubbed Maggot Mile by Florida state investigators who have cracked down on the Ponzi scheme businesses, the financially questionable companies that have built equally glitzy offices there. Globe Communications is not such a business: published figures estimate annual revenue to be $38 million, and Phil Bunton acknowledges that that was ballpark (*The Enquirer/Star* group is larger by a factor of seven. Its total revenues last year were $283,709,000). Globe Communications is nestled into a corporate park, across the street from Siemens, near IBM. Behind the obligatory jungle of plants, its stagy entrance is set off by a waterfall and an outlandish bronze Atlas, modesty paneled, holding a huge see-through globe of the world.

I had talked with Phil Bunton, *WWN*'s first editor, in his office at Globe the day before. In former days staffers of the competing tabloids drifted from one to the other, ratcheting up their salaries with each move and changing jerseys in the cricket matches the two companies played against each other. Americans are beginning to replace the rogue British journalists, and bowling is now the competitive sport of choice between the two more stable staffs. Phil, a veteran of those days, is a portly, pinkly affable Scotsman with sandy hair. His eyes twinkle behind his glasses. He is a former Fleet Street journalist who began his newspapering life as a farm editor in the north of Scotland. He came to the United States in 1973 to work on the *Star*, started by Rupert Murdoch, as did many other British reporters and editors. The *Globe*, the eldest of the publications in the corporation, which is still Canada-based, was spun out of a Montreal entertainment magazine in the 1960s by the magazine's accountant, Mike Rosenbloom. Rosenbloom, still the owner, continues to live in Montreal, but moved the editorial offices to Boca Raton to take advantage of the Florida pool of British talent (100,000 came in the last decade alone), many of whom moved there for one reason or another, climate and good money among them.

I asked Phil how it was that the British have become so successful in American journalism. Not only have they dominated the tabloids, but some of our most upscale magazines, *The New Yorker* and *Vanity Fair*, *National Review*, *TV Guide*, *Details*, and *Harper's Bazaar*, have all begun to be edited by Brits. British writers are becoming stars on many magazines and British editors are sought for our publishing houses. "Yes," Phil replied, smiling broadly. "It's nice for us. We've become the Flavor-of-the-Month," and he went on to explain:

I think Brits have a talent that has died out in this country, a talent for sensationalizing, for giving, intuitively, the audience what it wants, rather than trying to educate. We give them scandal and gossip. I think most American journalists take themselves far too seriously and regard themselves as being crusaders, as if they are really out to improve the world. *We* know it's a business, and writers for *The New York Times* don't seem to believe that somebody upstairs in accounting is actually counting money and trying to improve profits for next year.

But he has also been happy to have the protection of the First Amendment, which acknowledges the specialness of the American press business. In recent years no other *Globe* story has attracted more attention than the one in which it named the woman in the William Kennedy Smith rape case. Once her name was in print, the soberer media, *The New York Times* and NBC among them, used her name, too. "We got hauled into court," Phil said. "Florida has a rape-victim/shield law that we argued was unconstitutional. The local court supported us. It was a First Amendment case."

Recent court cases have made tabloid editors more cautious, and all have attorneys who vet every issue, but the multimillion dollar suits for slander and defamation by celebrities such as Frank Sinatra, Cary Grant, and Carol Burnett are often settled out of court or, in the end, reduced on appeal. In the famous Carol Burnett case against the *National Enquirer,* the star's $1.6 million judgment was reduced to $200,000 on appeal. And ordinary people, with private lives to defend, fare no better. Nellie Mitchell, a ninety-six-year-old Arkansas woman, falsely identified by *Sun* as a 101-year-old pregnant mail carrier, won a judgment of $1.5 million in state court, but the federal appeals judge has ordered the sum reduced, and the case, Phil told me, is still in process.

When the tabloids want a story or a picture, they are willing to pay for it. *Star,* the Tarrytown, N.Y.–based part of the *Enquirer/Star* group, paid $150,000 to Gennifer Flowers for her claim that she had had an affair with Bill Clinton, a story that swirled around the candidate when he was in the New Hampshire primary. Phil told me:

Maybe 20 percent of our stories in *Globe* are purchased, but scandals don't actually sell many issues. [About the same time *Star* was working on the Gennifer Flowers story] we were working on one about [another woman whom Clinton was rumored to know.] The bizarre thing is that Gennifer Flowers didn't add one sale to the *Star* and our story didn't make one extra sale for us. In fact both of us lost sales that week. . . . We broke our stories too early. Clinton was just one of the pack then. The real advantage would have been if we could have kept the story for half a year and run it the month before the election, but you're scared to sit on a story for that long.

Iain Calder, another Scotsman, known as the Ice Pick ("at least I stab them in the ribs instead of behind their backs") is editor of the *National Enquirer* and president of National Enquirer, Inc. He would not grant me an interview. I did peek, however, as I walked through the *National Enquirer* newsroom on my way to the *WWN* alcove. "I *do* hope you don't think I am being rude," Calder had purred to me over the telephone, "but I wouldn't like to be put in the tabloid context," and went on to add:

Well, of course, we *are* a tabloid, but I like to compare us to *People* magazine. Do you know, last week we ran the same picture of Princess Di that *People* did? Not just like it, but the *very* same . . . Of course, I'd be happy to talk with you, open the files, everything, if you'd write a story exclusively about the *National Enquirer.*

The *National Enquirer,* in its logo, states that it has "the largest circulation of any paper in America," and the corporate annual report lists it as second only to *TV Guide* in sales at "supermarkets and other retail outlets." These are, again, tabloid truths. And it is true that tabloid readers themselves commonly refer to them as "papers," but ABC considers all six supermarket tabloids, including the *National Enquirer*, to be magazines, and the California court, ruling in the Burnett case, agreed. Checking the ABC figures cited above, the *National Enquirer* is fourteenth in U.S. sales. (The leader is *Modern Maturity* with a circulation of 22,450,000.) *National Enquirer*, with sales of 3,706,030, is approximately 400,000 ahead of the eighteenth-placed *People*, to which Iain Calder would prefer to be compared. The circulation figures of the *National Enquirer*, along with the other supermarket tabloids, show a steady decline over the past several years, according to ABC figures.

Staffers at the tabloids attribute shrinking sales to a variety of causes: the recession, competition from lottery tickets at the checkout stand, tabloid television, the increasingly juicier content of the mainstream press ("Look at *The New York Times* getting into the Woody Allen mess," Phil Bunton said gleefully). But all of them are victims of the success of their own distribution systems. In Pope's day, the sales force that he employed to put the *Enquirer* into supermarkets handled his tabloids exclusively. But after his death his publications and sales organization, Distribution Services, Inc., were purchased for $412 million by a New Yorker, Peter Callahan. Callahan, a man who makes money by buying and selling magazines, was then head of a small company, the eponymous MacFadden Holdings, containing the remnants of the publishing empire of Bernarr MacFadden, the physical culturist who brought demotic journalism to the masses. In 1990 Callahan also bought *Star* for $400 million and the following year the *Star/Enquirer* group was reorganized as a public stock company within Callahan's purview. "What Mr. Callahan did," Anna Blanco, spokeswoman for MacFadden Holdings, told me on the telephone, "was to recognize the potential of Distribution Services, Inc., DSI. Through it we now distribute lots of other magazines to the supermarkets, not just the tabloids. It's a real moneymaker."

Globe has a similar distribution setup and so all the tabloids must compete with other colorful and titillating magazines at the counter.

Will it be the *Cosmopolitan* girl with her cleavage? *TV Guide*? *Good Housekeeping*, with its promise of a better life? Or FARMER SHOOTS 23 LB. GRASSHOPPER? More and more, the competition also includes other in-house publications produced to increase total corporate revenue, special issues as well as trial publications relating to health, soap opera, country-and-western music. "Pope was right not to allow distribution of other magazines," said a well-positioned staffer who spoke on condition of anonymity. "Now we're just fighting for rack space with all the other clients of DSI."

"It always struck me as ridiculous," Phil Bunton told me, "that Generoso Pope never got credit for revolutionizing a segment of the magazine business in this country. He made the tabloids what they are, brought them into the supermarkets and, as a result, other magazines came into the supermarkets which were never there before."

Generoso Paul Pope, Jr., born in 1927, was a bright young man who graduated from Massachusetts Institute of Technology at the age of nineteen. After a desultory few years working in the family sand-and-concrete business, his father's newspaper *Il Progresso*, and even a short stint with the CIA, he assembled enough borrowed money to buy, in 1952, the ailing *New York Enquirer*, a weekly tabloid newspaper with a circulation of only 17,000. "I spent the next six years going around borrowing money," Pope told an interviewer before his death, recollecting those days. "I became the world's expert check-kiter." He filled the pages of the *Enquirer* with blood, sex, violence, and big headlines (PASSION PILLS FAN RAPE WAVE) and circulation did begin to increase. In 1957 he renamed it *National Enquirer* and began to dream of a readership of 20 million. By the late 1960s Pope was looking for sales outlets that would give his paper more potential buyers and reasoned that nearly everyone spends some time in the supermarket. It would be a lucrative item in grocery stores, where the profit margin is measured in a penny or two. (Today, with a cover price of ninety-nine cents, each copy of

National Enquirer sold makes the supermarket twenty-one cents, according to a DSI spokeswoman.) Supermarket executives were dubious, however, because of the generally sleazy reputation *National Enquirer* had earned. Pope cleaned up the content, stripped it of the worst of the gore and sex, brought in more celebrity gossip, introduced health features, contemplated the *Reader's Digest.* In 1971, the year he moved *National Enquirer* to Lantana, not far from the home he had purchased, he began using some highly placed influence to bring the supermarket executives around. Pope told an interviewer in 1983:

We got Melvin Laird, who was Secretary of Defense at the time, to personally take supermarket executives on a tour of the White House, where they spent half an hour with President Nixon. The guys who owned Winn-Dixie, which just wouldn't let us in nohow, walked out of that meeting and said "We still don't like the *Enquirer,* but we've got to put it in now."

Today, Laird remembers the meeting a little differently, says that Nixon appeared quite accidentally, but he admits that one of his aides, Dan Henkin, Assistant Secretary of Defense, had arranged for Pope to attend a Pentagon briefing to supermarket executives during a convention they were holding in Washington. Laird, who spoke at the briefing, had then invited them on the White House tour. Pope had been coy in the 1983 interview about his connection with Laird. "It's politics," Pope said. "One hand washes the other."

And so, early in the 1970s, *National Enquirer* followed *Woman's Day* into the supermarkets, nuzzling aside the candy bars and razor blades at the checkout counter, a place where Americans wait in line, staring into space, taking in whatever is able to engage their attention. In its best years, a decade straddling the 1970s and 1980s, the *Enquirer* could sell 5 million copies a week, a figure short of Pope's dream of 20 million, but still enough to make him a wealthy man. When he died in 1988, his personal fortune was estimated to be $150 million. Pope, who had loved his work, read every word in his tabloids, worked in the office seven days a week, sometimes in bathing suit and carpet slippers, often with opera playing as background music, watching, perhaps, for the three topics reporters said they could never write about: the CIA, the Mafia, and Sophia Loren. He had been advised that he could have made even more money had he expanded and diversified. To such advice he replied, according to Eddie Clontz, "Yeah, but you can only eat so many hamburgers."

WWN, which Eddie considers to be the last of the genuine tabloid newspapers, with roots in nineteenth-century American journalism, was founded by Pope almost accidentally, an afterthought. The building circulation of *National Enquirer* during the 1970s had been so tempting to Rupert Murdoch, the Australian press baron, that he tried to buy it. Failing that, he began a new American tabloid in 1974, *Star*, the gossip-, scandal-filled, steamy tabloid based on the British model, in color. Pope, to meet the competition, was forced to switch from black-and-white to color printing, too. He believed that the market was good enough for another tabloid, so, in 1979, in order that his black-and-white presses did not stay idle, he began the *Weekly World News*. He filled it with leftover bits from *National Enquirer* and gave Phil Bunton the job of editing it. But the content was wrong and circulation began to fall. Eddie was hired in 1981. "We were the highest-paid journalists in the world—still are," he told me,

but Mr. Pope was a taskmaster and expected us to produce. The average tenure back then was about six months, so you were rich for half a year at least. He called us into the office and gave us six months to turn the paper around. Or *ffft!* to the paper and probably us.

With that deadline in mind, Eddie began to study the successful tabloids of the past and carefully crafted *WWN*—of which he became managing editor in 1982, editor in 1989—on their example, looking to William Randolph Hearst, Joseph Pulitzer, Bernarr MacFadden, and others as models.

In a sense, tabloids—that is, news in condensed form (the word "tabloid" was registered in 1884 as a trademark to describe condensed substances used in pharmacy)—have been with us in oral tradition ever since people began entertaining one another with ballads and popular stories. A seventeenth-century ballad told of a phantom drummer who threw children out of bed. The 10 November 1992 *Sun* features a story with pictures: YOUNG FAMILY FLED THEIR HOME IN HORROR AFTER A CHILD-HATING SPIRIT REPEATEDLY TERRORIZED THEIR LITTLE BOYS. Printing presses, once developed, were often used for single newssheets—broadsides—to satisfy a universal human desire to read about sensational events. An early broadside tells the story of one Mary Dudson, who swallowed a small snake that grew inside her and eventually killed her. In 1924, the *New York World* published a story about a girl who died and was found to be "harboring" a living snake that had hatched from an egg she had swallowed. *WWN* of 10 November 1992: X-RAY SHOWS LIVE SNAKE TRAPPED IN MAN'S STOMACH.

S. Elizabeth Bird, a cultural anthropologist, became fascinated with the way these folk stories repeated themselves, eventually writing *For Enquiring Minds* (1992), from which the above early examples are drawn. She studied tabloids as folklore, and noted their preoccupation with eternal themes: the hero who didn't die (Elvis, J.F.K., and Jimmy Hoffa are our current favorites); children raised by animals (remember Romulus and Remus?); ghosts (haunted toasters are big right now); monsters (Big Foot has replaced dragons); flying saucers (C. G. Jung once traced back the image of round, healing objects coming from the skies in times of social disruption to certain medieval paintings); fairy stories about princes and princesses (today's definition of royalty has been expanded to include Oprah Winfrey and Elizabeth Taylor).

Eddie agrees with Dr. Bird's analysis. He also points out "the misconception that a lot of journalists and academicians have that the tabloids were a British phenomena. They were not. Tabloids were really American. The wild and woolly papers of the 1800s were merciless, with scandal and all."

It is true, however, that in America the penny press had been as popular as it was in England. In 1845 the weekly national *Police Gazette,* which Simon Bessie in his classic *Jazz Journalism* terms "a trade organ of the Fast Life," showed American publishers what a market there was for lurid stories printed in tiny columns. By the turn of the century, Americans had given the world a new term, "yellow journalism," which served to identify the reckless content of newspapers such as Hearst's *New York Journal.* The *Journal* published the first comic strip, "The Yellow Kid," the star of which always wore yellow. But in the end the Brits must take the credit for pulling all the strands together and inventing the modern tabloid. Alfred Harmsworth, later Lord Northcliffe, saw as early as 1894 the potential of a small-format newspaper with brief, colorful stories and lots of pictures, ones that appealed to women as well as men. By 1909 his *London Daily Mail* and *Daily Mirror* were selling a million copies a day. Harmsworth eyed the American market and told Joseph Patterson of the *Chicago Tribune:* "If the rest of you don't see the light, I'll start one [a U.S. tabloid] myself." And so, in 1919, Patterson issued America's first true tabloid newspaper, *Illustrated Daily News,* fifteen inches by eleven inches, with a front page dominated by a photo of the Prince of Wales, who was soon to visit Newport; a back page featuring bathing beauties, and the pages in between stuffed with picture stories about "personalities" in the news. Imitators were immediate and many. Space here permits singling out only one, but it is one that influenced Eddie Clontz and Generoso Pope as well.

Bernarr MacFadden, 1868–1955, is remembered today as a body builder, health-food advocate, and inventor of Cosmotorianism, the happiness religion. But MacFadden also had a strong populist belief in the common man and a shrewd business sense; combined, these led him to establish such magazines as *True Story,* which endured to become the nub of Peter Callahan's MacFadden Holdings, Inc. In MacFadden's day *True Story* editors were taxi drivers and dime-store clerks who were ordered not to edit anything out of the confessions sent in by "ordinary" people. In 1924 he began the *New York Graphic,* a tabloid, on the same principle, enlisting whenever possible first-person participants to write the news (HE BEAT ME—I LOVE HIM) and advised his editors "Don't stick with the bare skeleton of the facts." In his first issue MacFadden told readers "We intend to interest you mightily. We intend to dramatize and sensationalize the news and some stories that are not new." With this in mind, MacFadden developed the composograph, a photograph that was enhanced, altered, sometimes posed. A composograph, for instance, enabled the *Graphic* to show the king of England scrubbing his back with a brush inside his own bathroom (tabloid pursuit of British royalty began long before Fergie and Di). In 1927 the *Graphic* brought both embellishment and the composograph into the famous divorce case of a teenage wife and her wealthy, publicity-hungry husband. The story of "Peaches" Heenan and "Daddy" Browning may be nearly seventy years old, but the treatment is as up-to-date as The Donald and Marla. I'll let Simon Bessie tell it:

Peaches's "private .diary" was serialized and countless intimate pictures were printed. Among the numerous composographs were several of the *Graphic*'s outstanding achievements in this line. Daddy and Peaches were shown playing "doggies" in their boudoir under the headline, WOOF, WOOF, I'M A GOOF. Daddy was persuaded to adopt an "African honking gander" as a pet and was pictured leading the bizarre animal about New York. The picture was captioned HONK, HONK IT'S THE BONK.

In the end, the Depression and the resultant change in the spirit of America killed the *Graphic,* which closed in 1932. But Eddie also points out that "sensational publications usually had a tremendous, meteoric rise and then a very precipitous fall." He regards it as his challenge to "take a paper in these times and sustain it as a sensational publication. Gossip, myth, mysteries. Those are all a part, and so is making it a forum for readers. Hearst," says Eddie admiringly, "was a master of that."

I talked to Elizabeth Bird by telephone, and she pointed out that anthropologists and cultural historians spend a lot of time trying to track down early versions of folkloric stories, and delight in finding a 200-year-old text. We find much of today's popular folklore in the tabloids, which are available to us everywhere: drugstores, supermarkets, newsstands, train stations—but only for one week at a time. And then it is gone, virtually untraceable for scholars 200 years hence. The State Historical Society of Wisconsin, home to the largest alternative press collection in the United States (4,000 titles), does not collect the supermarket tabloids. The Library of Popular Culture at Bowling Green University in Ohio collects only donated copies and has no complete runs. The New York Public Research Library is just beginning to assemble a collection of *National Enquirer* and *Star*, hopes to acquire back runs. The Library of Congress, which receives issues for copyright purposes, keeps current issues of five of them (*Sun* is discarded) and has microfilm of *National Enquirer* back to 1969. None of the tabloids is indexed, and all librarians contacted said they are beginning to receive research questions about material in the tabloids but have no way of helping, short of going through whatever issues they have page by page. Even comic books are better represented in many research collections. Folklorists of the future will not be able to read THE UNTOLD STORY: JERRY LEWIS' SECRET CANCER BATTLE, will never know that POPE SHARES PLANE WITH THE VIRGIN MARY or that JFK DID NOT DIE IN DALLAS.

On the day I visited the *National Enquirer* offices Eddie invited me to read his mail as he opened it. *WWN* had recently run a story about the fact, new to many of us, that there are baby ghosts. He tells me that the mail has been heavy from people who want to adopt them. And sure enough, letter after letter is from lonely, childless couples or single women, who describe, in detail, just how well-qualified they are to adopt a ghost baby. Eddie looks at me, seems touched, a trifle saddened. "We've had a thousand of these letters. Biggest response I've had in a year."

I look around the newsroom at reporters tapping their word-processor keys, peering into computer screens. I feel disoriented. I don't know what all of this means. And, oh yeah . . . the alien never made it. Terrible disappointment.

(October 1993)

FIVE

The Vicksburg Ghost

*The human predicament is typically
so complex that it is not altogether clear
which lies are vital and what
truths beg for discovery.*

—Vital Lies, Simple Truths:
The Psychology of Self-Deception,
by Daniel Goleman

I guess most people found it hard to believe that Elvis Presley didn't die after all but instead is alive and well and shopping at Felpausch's Supermarket, in Vicksburg, Michigan. I know I did when I read about it in *The New York Times* last fall. The *Times* wasn't on record as saying, THE KING LIVES, or anything like that, but it did report that a Vicksburg woman named Louise Welling had said she'd seen him the year before, in the supermarket's checkout line. Her sighting encouraged Elvins everywhere, many of whom believe that Presley faked his death. It also added an extra fillip to Elvismania, which is part nostalgia and part industry, the industry part consisting of the production of Elvis memorabilia, books, articles, tours, and prime-time TV "docudramas." Fans have made periodic demands for an Elvis postage stamp, and a multimedia musical—*Elvis: A Rockin' Remembrance*—had an Off-Broadway run this summer.

Promotion was what made Elvis Presley. In 1977, the year of his death, his likeness was more widely reproduced than any other save that of Mickey Mouse, and it has been reported that the news of his demise was greeted by one cynic with the words "Good career move!" According to Albert Goldman, the biographer who tells this story, Presley was by then a porky, aging, drug-befuddled Las Vegas entertainer and was getting to be a hard personality to promote. The Presley image shorn of the troublesome real man was easier to market. For example, after the King's death, Presley's manager, Colonel Thomas A. Parker, contracted with a vineyard in Paw Paw, Michigan—a town not far from Vicksburg—to produce a wine called Always Elvis. Its label bears a head shot of the entertainer, in a high-collared spangled white shirt, singing into a hand-held microphone. Colonel Parker's own four-stanza poem appears on the back of the bottle. Goldman has computed that the poem earned Parker twenty-eight thousand dollars in royalties, "making him, line for line, the best-paid poet in the world." Although the wine is no longer produced, I was able to find a dusty old bottle in my local liquor store. In the interests of journalism, I sampled it. It was an adequate companion to the poem, which closes with the couplet

> We will play your songs from day to day
> For you really never went away.

In its year-end double issue, *People* ran a story featuring recent photographs of Elvis purportedly taken by readers around the country, each picture as vague and tantalizing as snapshots of the Loch Ness monster. While debate mounted over whether or not Elvis Presley was still alive, I got stuck back there in the part of the *Times* story which said that he was shopping at Felpausch's. By the latter part of the 1950s, when Elvis arrived to sweep away the dreariness of the Eisenhower years, I was too old to respond to the Dionysian sexual appeal that he had for his teenage maenads; consequently, I was also unmoved by retro-Elvis. But I did grow up near Vicksburg. My family lived in Kalamazoo, a bigger town (in which Elvis was also said to have appeared) twelve miles to the north, and we spent our summers at a lake near Vicksburg. My widowed mother now lives at the lake the year round, and when I visit her I often shop at Felpausch's myself. I know Vicksburg tolerably well, so when I read the account in the *Times* I strongly suspected that the reporter had been snookered by a group of the guys over at Mar-Jo's Café, on Main Street, half a block from Felpausch's, which is on Prairie Street, the town's other commercial thoroughfare. Last June, while I was visiting my mother, I decided to drive into Vicksburg and find out what I could about the Elvis Presley story.

Vicksburg is a pretty village of two thousand people, more or less. A hundred and fifty years ago, when it was first settled by white people, the land was prairie and oak forest. James Fenimore Cooper, who lived for a time in the nearby town of Schoolcraft, wrote about the area in his book *Oak Openings*. It is in southern Michigan, where the winters are long and gray, and even the earliest settlers complained of the ferocity of the summertime mosquitoes. Vicksburg's one-block commercial section has been spruced up in recent years. There are beds of petunias at the curb edges, and new façades on the nineteenth-century buildings. The carefully maintained Victorian houses on the side streets are shaded by maples big enough to make you think elm. A paper mill, built near a dam that the eponymous John Vickers constructed on Portage Creek for his flour mill, has long provided employment for the local people, but today the village has become something of a bedroom community for commuters to Kalamazoo. Still, it seems very like the place I knew when I used to come to band concerts on Wednesday evenings at the corner of Main and Prairie, during the summers of the thirties and forties. The band concerts are a thing of the past, but there are other homegrown entertainments, such as the one going on the week I was there—the annual Vicksburg Old Car Festival, which is run by

Skip Knowles, a local insurance man. The festival has a fifties theme, and last year, inspired by the commotion that Louise Welling's sighting of Elvis had produced, Knowles added an Elvis-look-alike contest to the roster of events. Knowles has his office in a storefront on Main Street which used to be Matz's Confectionery, where I first discovered lime phosphates (known locally as "green rivers").

And the teenagers are still bored. While I was in the library going through back issues of local newspapers, two high school girls introduced themselves to me, saying that they had lived in Vicksburg all their lives and would be happy to talk to me about it. I asked them what they thought about Elvis Presley. They smiled patronizingly and informed me that no one they knew paid any attention to him. "But *everything* just stands still in Vicksburg," one of them confided. "We go to Kalamazoo on Saturday nights. I can't wait to get out of here and go to college."

Mar-Jo's has stayed the same, too. It has been in the same place for forty years. It was named after Marge Leitner and her partner, Josephine, whose last name no one at the café can remember. It is your basic tan place: tan floor, tan walls, tan tables, tan counter. The sign taped to the cash register was new to me. It said:

> THIS IS NOT
> BURGER KING
> YOU GET IT
> MY WAY
> OR YOU DON'T
> GET IT
> AT ALL

But the men having coffee together at the big round table near the front windows could have been the same ones sitting there the last time I was in, which was a couple of years ago.

"How's you-know-who?" gray crewcut asks feed-store cap. "Don't see her anymore."

The others guffaw, and one says, "He's taken her clothes."

"What clothes?" feed-store cap shoots back. A ripple of caffeine-fueled laughter circles the table.

Shirley White, a small, wiry woman, has been a waitress at Mar-Jo's for eleven years. Her hair is dark and tightly curled. She is efficient and cheerful. She knows virtually all her customers by name and how they like their coffee, and she banters with all of them. She gets to work at four-forty-five every morning, so she is usually way ahead of the best of the town wits, giving as good as she gets. The coffee-club boys once arranged the kind of prank on her that made me suspect them of the Elvis Presley caper. One of the regulars was a big man whom she could deftly unsettle with a clever phrase or two. His invariable riposte was a mumbled "Paybacks are hell." A few years ago, he was on vacation in Florida when her birthday came around, and she had nearly forgotten about him. Mar-Jo's was jammed that day, and no one would tell her why. "Just as I was busiest, this really big monkey walked in," she told me. "At least, it was a big guy dressed in a monkey costume, and he kept following me around, getting in my way. I was real embarrassed, and everyone kept laughing. Then a messenger handed me something called an Ape-O-Gram. It had just three words: 'Paybacks are hell.' "

Nearly all the coffee drinkers thought that the Elvis Presley sighting was as funny as the Ape-O-Gram, but no one would own up to having had a hand in making up the story. Louise Welling, it seemed, was a real person, and well known in town. She lived to the east, a few miles outside the village, they told me. "She's different, that's for sure," one of the coffee drinkers said. "No one believes her about Elvis Presley, but we all enjoyed it. Kind of put Vicksburg on the map. Isn't it funny? Elvis Presley wasn't even a very good singer. But I don't think Louise thinks it's funny." They referred me to a woman in town who knew Louise Welling better than they did and lived not far from her.

I went over to see the woman, who had an office in town, and talked to her with the understanding that her name would not be used. "Yes," she said. "I guess you could say that Louise is different. Her whole family is different, except for her husband, who works at General Motors. He's real quiet. But she's not crazy or anything. In fact, I think she's real bright. I don't know what to make of her claim that she saw Elvis Presley. She was a big Elvis fan from way back, but she doesn't bring him up or talk about this stuff unless someone asks her. She's a kind woman. She's reliable, too, and I wouldn't hesitate to call her if I had trouble. I'm afraid that after the story came out a lot of people played jokes on her. Made Elvis phone calls. Sent her Elvis letters. I'm pretty sure she's not in it for money. She just seems to think it's an interesting story, and it makes her mad when people don't believe her. Of course, none of us do. I don't know anyone in this town who thinks she really saw Elvis Presley. She was furious with the Vicksburg newspaper because they wouldn't run her story."

It seemed odd to me that the Vicksburg *Commercial* had not used Louise Welling's story—a story that had made *The New York Times*—so I called up Jackie Lawrence, the owner of the *Commercial*, and asked her to meet me for lunch at Mar-Jo's. Jackie Lawrence, a former nurse, is a big woman with curly brown hair, and she smiles a lot when she talks about Vicksburg, her adopted town. There are, she said, perhaps a dozen loyal Elvis fans in town—people who make pilgrimages to Graceland and would *like* to believe Louise Welling even if they don't.

We studied the daily specials, which were posted on the wall, and I decided to order Ken's Homemade Goulash. Next to the list of specials were snapshots of Ken Fowler, a cheerful young man with a fine brushy mustache, who bought Mar-Jo's two years ago and does a lot of the café's cooking. Shortly after he bought the place, he had a birthday, and the regulars, the waitresses, and Ken's wife conspired to bring in a belly dancer. The event was captured on film, and the posted snapshots show Ken, in apparent embarrassment, on a chair in one corner of the café, surrounded by laughing customers as a woman in gold draperies writhes in front of him.

Jackie Lawrence told me that she remembered Louise Welling coming into the newspaper office, which is a few doors down from Mar-Jo's, in March 1988, six months after the sighting at Felpausch's. At the time of her visit, Mrs. Welling knew that her story would soon be printed nationally, in the *Weekly World News*—and so it was, three months later. (According to Jim Leggett, who is the dean of freelance tabloid photo-journalists and once schemed to drill a hole in Howard Hughes's coffin in order to photograph his face, the *Weekly World News* is not exactly esteemed in the trade. "It prints the flotsam left by the better tabloids," he told me.) Mrs. Welling had wanted the *Commercial* to run her story first, Lawrence said. "She stood right by my desk, trying to tell me all about it. I said to her, 'I'm sorry, I don't have time for this,' and showed her out the door. And if she came in again, I'd say the same thing."

There was only one mention in the *Commercial* of the stir caused by Louise Welling's encounter with Elvis. The winner of Skip Knowles's 1988 Elvis-look-alike contest, a truck driver named Ray Kajkowski, came into the newspaper office a few days after the event to ask for prints of any pictures that might have been taken. While he was there, he kissed Jean Delahanty, one of the *Commercial*'s reporters, and she wrote a column about it, which concluded, "Some days are better than others!"

There is no chamber of commerce, as such, in Vicksburg. The town doesn't need one; it has Skip Knowles. I had telephoned Knowles before coming to Vicksburg. "Give me a jingle when you get in," he said. "Maybe we can do lunch." He is a handsome, trim, dark-haired man, and at our lunch a gold chain showed through the open collar of his shirt. There was another gold chain around his wrist. He was born in Atchison, Kansas, he told me, but spent his teenage years—from 1962 to 1968—near Detroit, where he developed a passion for cars and for cruising, that cool, arm-on-the-window, slow patroling of city streets which was favored by the young in those days. His dark eyes sparkled at the memory.

"We had what we called the Woodward Timing Association," he said. "It was made up of the guys that cruised Woodward Avenue. The Elias Big Boy at Thirteen Mile Road and Woodward was the place we'd go. But you know how the grass is always greener somewhere else? Well, my ultimate dream was to cruise the Sunset Strip. It wasn't until I got married, in 1969, and went out to California that I got to do that. And I talked to those guys cruising the Strip, and you know what they told me? It was *their* dream to cruise Woodward." He shook his head and laughed. "My wife and I still cruise when we go to a city." He hoped the local people had got cruising down pat for this year's festival, he said, handing me a packet of publicity material and a schedule of festival events. "I had to *teach* them how to cruise last year, which was the first time we closed off the streets for it."

The second annual Elvis-look-alike contest would be held at 9:00 P.M. Saturday, over on Prairie Street, in the parking lot of the Filling Station, a fast-food restaurant across the street from Felpausch's. Skip Knowles knew a good thing when he had it. Before last summer, he said, the festival had been drawing several thousand people, but each year he had had more trouble getting good publicity. "I can't understand the way they handled the Elvis business over at Felpausch's," he told me. "They even refused an interview with *The New York Times*. But I decided to play it for whatever it was worth."

After the first Elvis-look-alike contest, Knowles received a lot of calls from Louise Welling, who wanted to talk about Elvis Presley with him. "I put her off," he said. "She's *really* different. I think she really believes Presley never died." He also received other phone calls and visits. When his secretary told him last fall that a reporter from the *Times* was in his outer office waiting to talk to him, he thought it was just a hoax—a joke like the ones dreamed up at Mar-Jo's. But when he came out the man introduced himself as the paper's Chicago bureau chief and interviewed him about the Elvis contest. Then a producer from Charles Kuralt's show, *Sunday Morning,* called and said he was interested in doing a segment for the show on the impact of the Elvis sighting in Vicksburg, and would anything be going on in Vicksburg around Thanksgiving time? "I told him, 'Look, I'll do *anything* to get you here,' " Knowles recalled. " 'If you want me to rent Cadillac limos and parade them up and down Main Street for you to film, I'll get them.' But the TV people never came."

I decided that it was time to talk to Louise Welling herself. I couldn't make an appointment with her by telephone, because she had recently obtained an unlisted number, but one midweek morning I took a chance on finding her at home and drove out to see her. The Wellings live in the country, in a modest split-level house on non-split–level terrain; this is the sandy, flat part of Michigan, too far south for the ice-age glaciers to have sculpted it. Mrs. Welling sometimes works as a babysitter, but this morning she was home, along with four of her five children—all of them grown—and Nathan, her four-year-old grandson. Mrs. Welling is a heavyset woman with closely cropped dark hair and a pleasant face. Her eyes stay sad when she smiles. She touched my arm frequently as we talked, and often interrupted herself to digress as she told me her story. She said that she grew up in Kalamazoo and for a time attended St. Mary's, a Catholic grammar school there. When she turned sixteen, she was given a special present—a ticket to a Presley concert in Detroit. "Somehow, the fellow who took tickets didn't take mine, so after the first show I was able to move up, and I sat in front during the second," she said. "And then, toward the end, Elvis got down on his knee right in front of me and spread his arms wide open. Well, you can imagine what *that* would be like for a sixteen-year-old girl." Her voice trailed off, and she fell silent, smiling.

I asked her if she had continued to follow his career.

"When I got married, I started having children, and I never thought much about Elvis," she said. "After all, I had problems of my own." But then, in 1973, she saw a notice in a throwaway shopping newspaper from Galesburg, a nearby town, saying that Presley would be in Kalamazoo and, although he would not be performing, would stay at the Columbia Hotel there.

"I didn't try to get in touch with him," Mrs. Welling said, adding, with a womanly smile, "I had a husband, and you know how that is." Three years later, however, Presley appeared in concert in Kalamazoo, and she sent flowers to him at the Columbia Hotel, because she assumed that he would be staying there again. She went to the concert, too, and, as she remembers it, Elvis announced in the course of it that he had a relative living in Vicksburg. "He said he liked this area," she recalled. "Kalamazoo is a peaceful place. He'd like that. And I think he's living at the Columbia right now, under another name. But they won't admit it there. Every time I call, I get a runaround. You know what I think? I think he has become an undercover agent. He was interested in that sort of thing."

"What year was it that you saw him in concert in Detroit?" I asked. I had read somewhere that Presley had not started touring outside the South until 1956.

"Oh, I don't remember," Mrs. Welling said. "I'm fifty-one now, and I had just turned sixteen—you figure it out."

The arithmetic doesn't work out—nor, for someone who grew up in Kalamazoo, does the Columbia Hotel. The Columbia had its days of glory between the First World War and Prohibition, and it was growing seedy by the forties, when I used to ride by it on my way to school. Its decline continued after I left Kalamazoo, until—according to Dan Carter, one of the partners in a development company that remodeled the hotel to create an office complex called Columbia Plaza—it became "a fleabag flophouse and, for a while, a brothel." Carter also told me that in the mid-eighties a rumor arose that Elvis Presley was living there, behind the grand pink double doors on the mezzanine, which open into what was once a ballroom. The doors have been locked for years—the empty ballroom, its paint peeling, belongs to the man who owns Bimbo's Pizza, on the floor below—but that didn't deter Elvins here and abroad from making pilgrimages to Columbia Plaza. "You'd hear foreign voices out in the hallway almost every day," he said. "Then there was a visit from some people from Graceland—at least, they told us they were from Graceland, and they looked the part—who came by to see if we were making any money off this." They weren't, he said, and today the building's management denies that Elvis Presley, under any name, lives anywhere on the premises.

Mrs. Welling's next good look at Elvis Presley came at Felpausch's, in September 1987. There had been, she told me, earlier hints. In 1979, she had seen a man in the back of the county sheriff's car when the police came to her house to check on the family's dog, which had nipped a jogger. "The man in the back seat was all slouched down, and he didn't look well," she said. "I'm sure it was Elvis." A few years later, black limousines began to appear occasionally on the road where she lives. "Now, who around here would have a limo?" she asked. Then she began seeing a man she believes was Elvis in disguise. "He looked real fake," she recalled. "He was wearing new bib overalls, an Amish hat, and a beard that didn't look real. I talked to a woman who had seen the same man, and she said he sometimes wore a false nose. Now, why does he have to bother with disguises? Why couldn't he have said that he needed a rest, and gone off to some island to get better?"

A note of exasperation had crept into Mrs. Welling's voice. She showed me a cassette that she said contained a tape that Presley made after he was supposed to have died; in it, she said, he explained why he had faked his death. But when she played it the sound was blurred and rumbly, and I couldn't make out the words. The tape had been issued in 1988, to accompany a book by a woman—with whom Mrs. Welling has corresponded—who put forward the theory that the body buried as Presley's was not his own. The book and another by the same author, which Welling said was a fictional account of a rock star who fakes his death, were lovingly inscribed ("It's hard to take the heat") to Mrs. Welling.

Here is what Mrs. Welling said happened to her in September 1987. She had just been to eleven-o'clock Sunday Mass at St. Martin's Church. With grandson Nathan, she stopped at Felpausch's to pick up a few groceries. Having just celebrated one publicly accepted miracle, she saw nothing strange in the private miracle at the supermarket.

"The store was just about deserted," she said. "There wasn't even anyone at the checkout register when I went in. But back in the aisles I felt and heard someone behind me. It must have been Elvis. I didn't turn around, though. And then, when I got up to the checkout, a girl was there waiting on Elvis. He seemed kind of nervous. He was wearing a white motorcycle suit and carrying a helmet. He bought something little—fuses, I think, not groceries. I was so startled I just looked at him. I knew it was Elvis. When you see someone, you know who he is. I didn't say anything, because I'm kind of shy and I don't speak to people unless they speak first. After I paid for the groceries, I went out to the parking lot, but no one was there."

I asked Mrs. Welling if she had told anyone at the time what she had seen. She replied that she had told no one except the author of the Elvis-isn't-dead book, who was "very supportive." After that, she and her daughter Linda started seeing Elvis in Kalamazoo—once at a Burger King, once at the Crossroads Shopping Mall, and once driving a red Ferrari. And she said that just recently, while she was babysitting and filling her time by listening to the police scanner, she heard a man's voice ask, "Can you give me a time for the return of Elvis?" and heard Presley reply, "I'm here now."

I asked her what her family thought about her experiences. Linda, a pale, blond woman who was sitting off to one side in a dining alcove smoking cigarettes while I talked to her mother, was obviously a believer, and occasionally she interjected reports of various Elvis contacts of her own. "But *my* mother thinks it's all nutty," Mrs. Welling said, laughing. "She says I should forget about it. My husband doesn't say much—he's real quiet—but he knows I'm not crazy."

It wasn't until the spring of 1988, Mrs. Welling said, that she started getting in touch with the media. She claims that she didn't bother talking to the people at the Vicksburg newspaper (although Jackie Lawrence remembers otherwise), because "it wasn't an important newspaper." Instead, she tried to tell her story to the Kalamazoo *Gazette* and people at the television station there. No one would take her seriously—except, of course, the author of the Elvis book. After Mrs. Welling had written to her and talked to her on the telephone, a writer for the *Weekly World News* phoned for an interview. Mrs. Welling asked him how he knew about her, but he declined to reveal his sources. In early May, the tabloid prepared the ground for Mrs. Welling's story by running one that took note of the rumor that Presley was living in Columbia Plaza, and gave Mrs. Welling's friend a nice plug for her book. Shortly after that, the syndicated columnist Bob Greene gave the rumor a push. By that time, the Kalamazoo *Gazette* realized that it could no longer ignore Mrs. Welling's phone calls, and in its May 15 issue Tom Haroldson, a staff writer, wrote a front-page story headlined "ELVIS ALIVE" IN KALAMAZOO, SAY AREA WOMAN AND NEWS TABLOID. That was the beginning of Mrs. Welling's fame, but it was not until June 28 that the *Weekly World News* told her whole story. In thousands of supermarkets, the issue appeared with a big front-page picture of Mrs. Welling and a headline in type an inch and a half high proclaiming "I'VE SEEN ELVIS IN THE FLESH!" The story began to be picked up by newspapers around the country as a brightener to the increasingly monotonous accounts of the preconvention presidential campaigns. CBS investigated it for possible production on *60 Minutes*. Radio stations from coast to coast and as far away as Australia called to interview Louise Welling and anyone else they could find. Kalamazoo's mayor, Edward Annen, reacted to all this by announcing to a *Gazette* reporter, "I've told them that everyone knows this is where he lives and that they should send their residents here to spend tourist dollars to find him."

Funny signs sprouted throughout Kalamazoo and Vicksburg in places of commerce. A rival market of Felpausch's posted one that said JIMMY HOFFA SHOPS HERE. A dentist boasted ELVIS HAS HIS TEETH CLEANED HERE. At Mar-Jo's, the sign read ELVIS EATS OUR MEATLOAF. The folks at Felpausch's, however, were not amused. Cecil Bagwell, then the store's manager, told the *Gazette*, "The cashier who supposedly checked out Elvis that day cannot remember anything about it," and characterized Mrs. Welling as "an Elvis fanatic." Bagwell no longer works at Felpausch's, but I spoke with Jack Mayhew, the assistant manager, who scowled when I brought up the subject. "I won't comment," he said, adding, nonetheless, "We've never given the story to anyone, and we're not going to. All I'll say is that the woman is totally—" and he rotated an extended finger beside his head.

Before I left Mrs. Welling that morning, I asked her why she thought it was that *she* had seen Elvis, when others had not—did not even believe her.

"I don't know, but the Lord does," she answered. "I'm a religious woman, and when things like this happen—that we don't understand—it just proves that the Lord has a plan."

The next day, a friend who had heard about my investigations telephoned to tell me that there had been an Elvis sighting just a week or so earlier, in Kalamazoo, at the delivery bay of the Fader Construction Company, which is owned by her family. She hadn't seen the man herself, she said, but the women in the office had insisted that the truck driver making the delivery was Elvis Presley. I suspected that it might have been Ray Kajkowski, winner of the Elvis-look-alike contest and kisser of Jean Delahanty. This turned out to be true. On Friday evening, at a run-through for the Old Car Festival's cruising event, I was introduced to Kajkowski by Skip Knowles, and Kajkowski confirmed that he had made quite a stir while delivering a shipment of concrete forms to Fader. He gave me his card—he has apparently made a second career for himself as an Elvis impersonator at parties and night clubs—and then he whipped out a pair of mirrored sunglasses, put them on, and kissed me, too. "Young, old, fat, skinny, black, white, good-looking, not so good-looking, I kiss them all," he said. "I'm a pretty affectionate fellow. I was raised in a family that hugged a lot."

Ray Kajkowski lives in Gobles, not far from Vicksburg. At forty-one, he is thick-featured, a bit on the heavy side, and looks like—well, he looks like Elvis Presley. He has big sideburns and dyed black hair, which he wears in a pompadour. He went down to Graceland recently with his wife and his two teenage sons to study the Presley scene and recalls that while he was in the mansion's poolroom a couple came in and the wife took one look at him and collapsed on the floor in a faint.

"When I was growing up, I felt like an outsider," he told me. "I didn't think I was as good as other people, because my dad wasn't a doctor or a lawyer. We were just common folks. I knew about Elvis even when I was a little kid. I didn't pay much attention, though, except that some of my buddies had pictures of Elvis, so we'd trade those to our older sisters and their friends for baseball cards." He laughed.

"I felt like we were invaded when the Beatles came over," he continued. By that time—1963—he was at Central High School in Kalamazoo, and had begun to appreciate Presley's music and to defend it against foreign stars. "I mean, Elvis was a small-town boy who made good. He was just ordinary, and, sure, he made some mistakes, just like me or you or any of us. But he went from zero to sixty. He had charisma with a capital C, and somehow people still know it."

After Presley's death, Kajkowski said, he felt sad and started reading about Elvis and studying his old movies. "Then, in September or October 1987, right around then, I was at a 1950s dance in Gobles. My hair was different then, and I had a beard, but there was a fifty-dollar prize for the best Elvis imitator. Fifty bucks sounded pretty good to me, and I watched this one guy do an imitation, and he didn't move or anything, and I thought to myself, I can do better than that, so I got up and entered and won, beard and all. After that, I shaved off my beard, dyed my hair, and started building my act. I do lip-synch to Elvis tapes. I've got three suits now, one black, one white, one blue. My wife does my setups for me and runs the strobe lights. Evenings when we don't have anything else to do, we sit around and make scarves for me to give away. I cut them, and she hems them. When I'm performing, I sweat real easy, and I mop off the sweat with the scarves and throw them out to the gals. They go crazy over them. And the gals proposition me. They don't make it easy. Sometimes they rub up against me, and when I kiss them they stick their tongues halfway down my throat. Once I went over to shake the guys' hands, because I figured it was better to have them on my side. But one big guy wouldn't shake my hand, and later he came over and grabbed me like a grizzly bear and told me to quit it. 'You don't sound like Elvis Presley. You don't look like Elvis Presley. Stop it.' I told him, 'Hey, it's all lip-synch! It's just an act! It's entertainment!' But I try to keep it under control. My wife's the woman I have to go home with after the act."

I asked Kajkowski if he had ever been in Felpausch's. As a truck driver, he said, he had made deliveries there; occasionally, he even shopped there. But although he owned a motorcycle, he said, he rarely drove it, and he never wore a white motorcycle suit.

I asked him what he made of Mrs. Welling's story.

"Well," he said thoughtfully, "when someone puts another person at the center of their life, they read about him, they think about him, I'm not surprised that he becomes real for that person."

Saturday night, at nine o'clock, Louise Welling is standing next to me in the Filling Station's parking lot—it is built on the site of John Vickers's flour mill—in a crowd that has just seen prizes awarded in the fifties dance concert and is waiting for the beginning of the second annual Elvis-look-alike contest. She is neatly dressed in a blue-and-white checked overblouse and dark pants. Her hair is fluffed up, and she is wearing pretty pink lipstick. She invited me to come to the contest, and told me that although many of the entrants in such affairs didn't come close to Elvis she was hoping that this one would draw the real Elvis Presley out from hiding. "If he came to me in the past, I believe he'll come again," she said. "I hope it will be before I die. If he comes, I'm going to grab him and hold on to him and ask him why he couldn't just be honest about needing to get away for a rest. Why couldn't he just tell the truth? Look at all the trouble he's caused those who love him."

Earlier in the day, I stopped in at Mar-Jo's for coffee. There were lots of extra visitors in the café. Ken Fowler had turned on the radio to WHEZ, a Kalamazoo station, which was broadcasting live from out on the street, acting as the festival's musical host. Rock music filled the café. Patrons were beating time on their knees, and the waitresses had begun to boogie up and down behind the counter. I asked one of them—a girl named Laurie, who was decked out fifties style with a white floaty scarf around her ponytail—what she made of Mrs. Welling's story. "I think it's kind of fun," she said. "I haven't met the lady, but, you know, maybe she's right. After all, if Elvis Presley never died he has to be someplace."

Mrs. Welling is subdued, as she stands next to me, but all attention—scanning the people, anticipatory. We are at the very back of the good-natured crowd, which has enjoyed the nostalgia, the slick cars, the dances, the poodle skirts, and the ponytails. She spots Kajkowski and says to me that he's not Elvis but "so far he's the only one here who even looks anything like him."

Skip Knowles is up on the stage, in charge of what has turned out to be a successful event. There have been record-breaking crowds. Six hundred and fifty cars were entered. He has had plenty of media coverage, and he seems to be having a very good time. He calls for the Elvis contest to begin. Ray Kajkowski's act is so good now that he has no competition—he is the only one to enter. I watch him play the crowd. He had told me, "When I first started, I really liked the attention, but now it's just fun to do the show, and, yeah, I do get caught up in it. I like the holding power I have over people. I know how it is to feel left out, so I play to everyone. But I like people in their mid-thirties or older best. I don't like to entertain for these kids in their twenties. The gals back off when I try to drape a scarf around them. I think that's an insult." Now he is dancing around the edge of the crowd, reaching out to kiss the women, who respond to him with delight and good humor, and then he launches into what Mrs. Welling tells me is "You're a Devil in Disguise." I look at her, and she seems near tears. Her shoulders slump. "I don't like to watch," she says softly, and walks away to gather her family together for the trip home.

On my own way home, on the morning after the festival, I made one final stop in Vicksburg, on the south side of town, at what is left of Fraser's Grove. For about forty years—up until the early 1920s—Fraser's Grove was one of this country's premier spiritualist centers. In 1883, Mrs. John Fraser, the wife of a well-to-do Vicksburg merchant, turned the twenty-acre woodland into a camp and gathering place for mediums, believers in mediums, and the curious. She had been inspired by a lecture on spiritualism given in a hall on Prairie Street by one Mrs. R. S. Lily, of Cassadaga, New York, a town in the spiritually fervent "burned-over" district of that state. In the years that followed, Mrs. Fraser became a national figure in séance circles, and another resident of Vicksburg, C. E. Dent, was elected president of something called the Mediums' Protection Union. A group calling itself the Vicksburg Spiritualists was formed shortly after Mrs. Lily's visit, and it met each

Sunday. Its Ladies' Auxiliary held monthly chicken dinners (fifteen cents a plate, two for a quarter). On summer Sunday afternoons, people from around this country and abroad packed the campground at Fraser's Grove to talk of materialization and reincarnation and watch mediums go into trances to contact the dead. According to a 1909 issue of the Vicksburg *Commercial*, they debated subjects such as "Is the planet on which we live approaching final destruction, or is it becoming more permanent?" (A follow-up article reports that the Spiritualists opted for permanency.)

Trees still stand in much of Fraser's Grove, although some of them have been cut down to make room for a small housing development. The campground itself has been taken over by the Christian Tabernacle, which makes use of the old camp buildings. Tazzie, my German shepherd, was with me, and I parked at the edge of the grove to let her out for a run before we drove onto the interstate highway. We headed down a dim path, where events passing strange are said to have taken place. The grove produced no Elvis, no John Vickers, not even a phantom band concert or the apparition of Mr. Matz—no spirits at all. But Tazzie did scare up a rabbit, and the oaks were still there, and, untamed through a hundred and fifty generations, so were the mosquitoes.

(September 1989)

SIX

Driving
in Boston

Those of us who wander across this country—hard-core itinerants, escapees from a Stanley Elkin novel, a ragtag of peddlers, truckers, journalists, compulsive tourists—meet in flyspecked cafés off the interstates and gossip about the cities that are our temporary destinations.

Manhattan, the island borough of thirty-four square miles, the city that gave us gridlock, each day invites in 877,000 motorists and then does not let them park. Over our coffee we trade hints on what it is not too illegal to do with our delivery trucks there. We tell tales of cabbies and their refreshing obscenities.

Outside Dallas, Interstate 35 splits into two identically numbered segments, differentiated by a tiny W and E, which run north and south. Lulled by interstate monotony, the unwary sometimes fail to notice the split and circle the city on the 35s and their various permutations until they give up and opt for Waco. That furnishes the underpinning for the legend of the ghost of I-35. It is said in Western truck stops that once a young couple with a small child (some versions claim twin children) circled Dallas in July until their auto air conditioner failed and they died, and that on still nights, when the moon is full and there is a lull in traffic, you can hear the wail of a child.

Some say Nashville is the most testing city to drive in, but most say Boston. Boston because of its streets. Boston because of its drivers.

"Ah yes, Boston," says Mark, a photographer just returned from a job there. "Boston, the city where green means go and yellow means go a little faster."

A man from New York, a city not noted for its gentle traffic manners, tells of the time he lost a muffler on Storrow Drive to a Bostonian aggressively merging onto that thoroughfare. The Bostonian, despite the fact that he shed his own bumper in the clash, never glanced to either side and sped on when the New Yorker pulled over to exchange insurance information.

Boston drivers are steely, quick, opportunistic, decisive, but above all they do not look another driver in the eye. They probably do not drive as fast as we itinerants claim they do. A recent comparison showed that motorists in Columbus drive just as fast. However, in Columbus, everyone, including the outsiders, knows where he is going. In Boston, only the Bostonians do. That makes them seem to be going faster.

"The day is past when the out-of-town driver, lost on Boston's streets, was a good joke," said *The Boston Globe* in a recent series on traffic. "That confused visitor, halted in the middle of an intersection, is likely to be the direct cause of a traffic jam that extends several blocks. . . . Get some signs up—and make sure they are readable and make sense."

There are those who claim that Boston is a city designed by M. C. Escher, its maps labeled by Italo Calvino. Bostonians speak of a central artery that does not appear on maps or signs; of squares that are not square, not labeled, and not acknowledged by Rand McNally.

Boston is an old town, its narrow streets not neat grids like Kansas City's. The streets wind, end in cul-de-sacs, curve back on themselves, disappear, intersect by the sixes and sevens at rotaries. Their direction is fluid and changing. An outsider, carefully learning that Charles Street is one way this way, returns a year later to find it that way. Overhead traffic signs are terse, grudging, and lacking in true meaning. Street signs are usually placed only on cross streets, leaving unnamed the street upon which one is driving.

A world explorer, a man equally at home in the forests of New Zealand and the trackless Arctic tundra, tried to find his way in a rented car from Logan International Airport to the Royal Sonesta Hotel in Cambridge. Forced into a high-speed exit decision at a rotary, he soon realized that he had made a wrong choice. He was immediately and irretrievably lost because there were nothing but cross-street signs so he could not find where he was on the map clenched in his fist. Cursing the lack of street signs, he asked a cabbie for directions. The cabbie told him he could not explain how to get to the hotel, but for a fee he would lead him. Disgusted, the explorer drove on and, coming to a fire station, parked his rental car in the driveway and refused to move until the firemen agreed to tell him where he was.

What the explorer did not know was that cabbies routinely pilot the lost through Boston streets. Floyd is a truck driver who has been delivering Russell Stover candy to the same warehouse in Boston for fifteen years. "Tried it on my own a couple of times," he says. "I figured, hell, I can deliver in Nashville, which is impossible; I'll soon have Boston in my head. But I'd get to one of them damn rotaries and on to another, rear back and find myself at the first again. And then there was always that same underpass that was too low for my truck. I didn't know how I got to it. But there it was every time. I didn't know how *not* to get to it either. Never could figure the place out, so I just hire a cabdriver to take me in. Same as other truckers do."

A practiced Boston driver is unsuited for traffic elsewhere. A Bostonian confessed that the horror of Boston driving is so universal that it's like breathing: you almost cease to notice. When he was in Alabama recently, the drivers there seemed to him unbelievably courteous, deliberate, and careful. It got on his nerves. "Why don't they *drive*?" he asked his wife.

Boston driving skills and way-finding are very special. It is said that Boston's streets are laid out on seventeenth-century cow paths, therefore the way to drive in Boston is to think like a seventeenth-century cow. Nerveless. Placid—not too much though. Superb sense of direction.

There is an amusing bit of driving from Back Bay Station to South Station. It is hard to think about, impossible to describe, but if one doesn't study it too much and keeps hoofing along, everything comes out O.K.

Not even a Bostonian can give directions for driving from North Beacon Street to Davis Square in Somerville, but by replacing street names in the head with points of the compass, it can be done.

Being lost is a concept only, and not one helpful to apply in Boston. One drives and drives and then, suddenly, one is someplace better.

In a rest stop in Pennsylvania, Mildred and Jim are sitting at a picnic table eating oranges. They are on their way home to Oklahoma from a vacation trip East. Their car has a sticker saying JESUS LOVES COWBOYS . . . & COWGIRLS, TOO.

They have had a good holiday.

"The best part was Boston," says Jim. " 'Course it didn't seem that way at first."

Mildred adds, "We went there to look at the historic things, the Liberty Bell and all."

"No, sweetheart," Jim says gently. "The Liberty Bell is what we didn't see in Philadelphia."

"Well. Anyway. Those old places. We wanted to see them all in Boston, but we couldn't get to any of them. We drove around one whole day not finding anything until it got dark. Then we came to an old building that didn't have a real name. It just said HOTEL on a little bitty sign. It was real pretty inside. Filled with antiques. The hotel didn't have a restaurant, but the nice lady at the desk sent us next door to an old house up on a hill behind some shrubs. It didn't have any sign at all. Inside was a big room with lots of real old furniture. It was just beautiful. All the tables had crystal bowls filled with roses, and the food was the best we had anywhere. Everyone was so kind and polite and talked to us a lot. Told us a lot of interesting stuff. One lady said we were in some historic part of Boston, real old I guess. It was the high point of our trip. But we never knew where we were.

"I don't suppose you'd know where that was, would you?"

(July 1986)

SEVEN

Kegling

A friend of mine found these terrific shoes in a secondhand store, bowling shoes divided longitudinally by color: the outer half is red, the inner half is blue, and a stripe of white runs up from toe to tongue. They have a pair of crossed bowling pins on each heel and a pair of jingle bells wired onto the laces. The shoes weren't her size, but she bought them anyway, and then gave them to me, with a smile, when she found out they would fit me. I wear them a lot. I like to look down at them twinkling there on my feet; they make me feel like doing soft-shoe routines. I went out to dinner with friends the other evening, and we discovered that the shoes knew how to gallop, a skill we had learned in second-grade phys ed but had forgotten.

I was in St. Louis not long ago, and the shoes walked me right into the National Bowling Hall of Fame and Museum. It's across the street from Busch Stadium—a pudgy building of gray and pink pebbles firmly anchored on a triangular lot by a squat tower at each apex. Inside are three floors of bowling displays and trinkets, and eight functioning bowling lanes. St. Louisans rent the place after hours for parties. They hire a disk jockey and a caterer and spend the evening eating, dancing, looking at the exhibits, and riding the elevators, and when all else palls they bowl a few frames. Last year, more than two hundred events were held in the museum, including a fortieth-birthday party, a wedding reception, and a Bar Mitzvah.

The display area is along an easy ramp that spirals through the building, and on it I learned, from a diorama showing a slouch-faced humanoid dressed in hides and animal teeth, that the first bowler may have been a caveman tossing rocks. A glass case held reproductions of bowling pins from 5200 B.C., unearthed in Egypt by Sir Flinders Petrie. They looked like pointed darning eggs with flat bottoms. A panel showed two muscly Anglo-Saxons escaped from an opera stage and dressed in skins and horned caps; one was holding a thick cup of something refreshing, and the other, war ax strapped to his waist, was holding an immense skin ball over his head. According to the panel, the Brothers Grimm and the historian Wilhelm Pehle traced bowling back to a pre-Christian game in northern Europe called Steinstossen, which consisted of knocking down upright stones by throwing weapons at them. Pehle went on to link bowling to a church ritual among the northern tribes in which parishioners rolled a stone at a *Kegel*, or club used for self-defense, which they renamed *Heide*—the heathen, that which is pagan, the Devil. Toppling the *Heide* symbolized the slaying of Satan, according to St. Boniface, an eighth-century English missionary, who adapted the game for his flock.

Strong stuff! But my shoes jingled me on up the ramp and planted themselves in front of a diorama of Martin Luther bowling. There he is, life-size, in flowing black robes, a soft hat on his head, and with a sprightly touch of red at his throat. His feet are in the correct bowling stance, and his hand is back and curved over a ball, which he is about to throw at wooden pins. Two children crouch watching. Behind him are bowling banners. Martin Luther built a bowling alley for his family and household, and he wrote that he himself enjoyed rolling out a ball now and again.

Apparently all over Europe there were people having too much fun bowling, for eventually the Germans, the French, and the English all banned the game, ostensibly because it encouraged gambling and rowdyism, separated families, and lured men from the armies. But the laws made exceptions for the wealthy and the titled, and members of the lower orders found loopholes. Sly bowlers in England invented a game, not specifically banned by law, called Bubble the Justice, in which balls were rolled into shallow holes. The museum's message is that the urge to bowl is irrepressible and that all over Europe people went on bowling and called what they were doing by other names: *skales, loggats, kayles, closh, cloish, Platzbahnkegeln, quilles de neuf, skittles.*

In America, the English brought lawn bowling to Virginia. The Dutch brought ninepins to New York. At the end of the spiral ramp, I stopped to peer into a mutoscope, an elegant gilt-spangled, light-filled stand the size and roughly the shape of a large gumball machine—a turn-of-the-century penny-arcade version of the movies. It told the story of Rip Van Winkle on a roll of cards. When I turned the mutoscope's crank fast enough, Rip's diminutive friends spiritedly knocked down their ninepins. At an IBM terminal at the top of the museum, even I, a computer illiterate, could press enough keys to discover that no one in the town where I live has ever bowled a three-hundred, or perfect, game, but that in the town in which I was born five screenfuls of folks have. I knew none of them. I felt like Rip Van Winkle.

My shoes danced on through the Bowling Hall of Fame (dark, respectful, male) and the Women's Bowling Hall of Fame (light, cheerful, suggestive of cookies). The museum was funded by major donations from equipment manufacturers and the producers of those beverages usually associated with the sport, and also by donations from bowling associations, many of which raised their contributions through bake sales. I examined a bowling-shirt display, antique bowling pin, bowling in art and quilt and stein. I circled the bowling lanes (four modern and four nostalgic); I would have liked to use one of them, but my shoes reminded me I didn't know how. I admired the historic-beer-tray display and ended up at the world's only mobile bowling pin, built by Mike Skrovan, of Cleveland, Ohio, around the chassis of a 1936 Studebaker coupé.

On my way back out to the street, I waved to the young man at the visitors' desk.

"*Nice* shoes," he said, with a smile.

(January 1989)

EIGHT

Deliveries

When I come to New York, I stay at the Y.M.C.A. on Forty-seventh Street between Second and Third avenues. The Y is a liberal and welcoming sort of place. I am not Y, I am not M, I am not C, and yet I am allowed to stay there, and even use the swimming pool. The location is convenient. The place is clean and cheap: twenty-eight dollars a night. Of course, the rooms are small—the size I like to imagine monks' cells to be—but, after all, I'm only in my room to sleep. The bathrooms are shared, but that is rather Continental. And lots of Europeans stay there. In the elevators, I hear spirited conversations in a variety of tongues. I can also leave my delivery truck out in front, because the whole block is designated a truck-standing zone. I'm not sure how *long* I can leave it there. I once parked, went into the Y, checked in, unpacked, took a shower and washed my hair, and came out to find my truck unticketed. So a truck-standing zone is good for at least that long.

Another thing I like about the Y is that there is a Smiler's all-night deli just around the corner on Third Avenue, so when I get up, at five in the morning, I can walk over there, buy a cup of coffee to go, bring it back, and sit in my tiny little room and drink it while I plan my delivery route. I like to be over at Macy's loading dock, on Thirty-fifth Street, before six-thirty. The men who work there have all come in by then and are having their coffee and Danish, and they aren't yet exasperated, as they sometimes are after the big semis start to arrive. My truck is big as pickups go—it's a three-quarter-ton—but it's a lot smaller than a tractor-trailer rig, which is what most loading docks are set up for. My deliveries, of just a few cartons at a time, are a nuisance to most dock men. But at six-thirty the men at Macy's are still in a good mood. They let me back up to one of the bays. I put down my tailgate, which is several feet below the loading-dock level, and unload my cartons up onto pallets, which they will move with a forklift. In winter, it's still dark then, and I have to wander around the loading dock in golden lamplight to find someone who will sign my invoice and officially receive my delivery. He checks the purchase-order number and the department-destination number, stamps the invoice in several places, and scrawls his initials on it. I give him the duplicate copy, and in several weeks, perhaps a month or longer, I'll receive a check for what I've delivered.

If I'm not there by six-thirty, I go looking for the dispatcher, who has a booth on the street and is sometimes in it. The first time I delivered to Macy's, he noticed my Missouri license plates. With a sigh, he told me how much he missed his girlfriend, who lived in Kansas City and was stubborn about moving to New York to be with him. We talked about Missouri and the recalcitrance of lovers for a while. He helped me find a parking place and let me wheel my cartons up a walk-in ramp on my hand truck. He remembers me from year to year and always gives me a big hug.

After Macy's, I drive to Seventh, hang a left, turn left again on

Thirty-fourth, right on Broadway, and go speeding downtown to the World Trade Center. It's enormous fun to drive down Broadway at that hour of the morning. No one is about except other delivery drivers, and we all hustle right along, making every light, the big wheels of our trucks scarcely noticing the potholes. New York is dark, cozy, and ours at that time of day.

Deliveries for the World Trade Center are made underground, down a ramp off West Broadway, in a cavernous space with a dock running the length of it. At the entrance, a guard looks over my invoice, checks to see that I have commercial license plates, and waves me on to what he says is the appropriate area. I thread my way between big pillars, tractor trailers, and a few vans. After I'm parked, it gets confusing and uncomfortable. No matter what the outside temperature, it's warm and clammy there, and the air is bad. After I've loaded my cartons on my hand truck, I'm drenched in sweat. The rules change every time I go there. My deliveries end up in Inhilco's Big Kitchen, on the concourse, but sometimes I have to take my cartons up in the freight elevator all the way to an Inhilco storage room, on the 106th floor—the ride is so fast it makes my ears pop—and then trundle my hand truck around until I can find someone willing to sign for the delivery. If I'm lucky, though, I can leave the cartons down on the loading platform and one of the workers will take them up.

The workers are, for the most part, young men who speak little English. I speak little Spanish. Fortunately, they bring forth all their Latin courtesy for an older woman, and somehow, with many gestures and in phrases halfway between our languages, we communicate. They are always sweet and helpful, and do what they can to save me from lifting my cartons, which weigh forty pounds each. One day, I had been sent from one uncomprehending young man to another. My sweatshirt was soaked, my hair disheveled. I was tugging my hand truck behind me, clutching my invoice book to my chest. My purse dangled from my shoulder. A young man stopped me, his dark eyes melting with concern, to point out that my purse was unzipped and a twenty-dollar bill was hanging from it. "You must be careful in this big city," he said haltingly.

Balducci's is next. I've sold to Balducci's for years, and remember the first time, when Louis himself came out to the truck, which was triple-parked on Sixth Avenue, to dicker over the price and help unload the order. The store has grown too prosperous for that now. The stock is controlled by a computer, and I deliver to a storage area on Eleventh Street between First and Second avenues, where there are no spaces reserved for trucks unloading. So I have to double-park and block all the early-morning traffic behind me while I ring a concealed bell and wait for a man to open a heavy metal grillwork gate. He usually comes out to help me unload, however, and once the drivers of the cars trying to get through see what is happening they settle down to honking in only a perfunctory way.

Next, I head uptown, to deliver to Bloomingdale's and a number of small shops on the East Side. The traffic is beginning to pick up by then, but in my truck I am high above it and can plan my strategy, threading my way in and out, going as fast as possible to finish my deliveries before ten-thirty, when double-parking, even with blinkers flashing, becomes unconscionable.

The little shops usually take only one carton, and so those deliveries are quick if I plan my route carefully and avoid as much as possible the narrow cross streets. My fat truck can barely fit through them, and I have to suck in my mirrors (folding them back), pray to the trucking gods that a tank truck will not be delivering fuel oil, and squeeze by.

At Bloomingdale's, I leave my truck running on Fifty-ninth Street—its flashers going and tailgate down, so that the traffic wardens in brown can see what I am doing—while I go inside the gourmet-food store to find someone willing to authorize the delivery. After this person has satisfied himself of my good intentions, he opens a lock on a very heavy metal trapdoor on the sidewalk outside the Fifty-ninth Street entrance-way. I go back and tug it open, sometimes only with the help of a strong passerby. Then I slip my cartons down the chute. I try to close the trapdoor in a satisfactory way, but I often fail, and leave an edge sticking up. This makes the man inside exceedingly cross. He invariably reminds me that people could sue Bloomingdale's if they tripped over the door, and that it would be my fault.

The Bloomingdale's buyer once directed me to deliver to the ware-house, over in Long Island City. I changed my schedule around and, after driving down from Boston, on a wintry day, planned to stop at the warehouse before checking into the Y. After losing my way several times, I found the warehouse at about 1:00 P.M. and pulled into a line of small trucks and delivery vans. I waited for half an hour and nothing happened, so I got out and asked what the protocol was. The other drivers, all men—Haitians, Puerto Ricans, Italians, Jamaicans, and a black from southern Alabama—were helpful and friendly. They advised patience. They explained that I, like them, was a "straight trucker." (This refers to the way we back our trucks up. We do it straight; tractor-trailer rigs cut and bend.) There were a lot of loading bays, but only one for straight truckers. Each load had to be processed on a computer, whose speed was that of geological change, apparently—the lucky straight trucker who was now at the bay had been there nearly an hour and had only three pieces to unload.

A Jamaican driver explained that he had been waiting since eight in the morning and had just a single carton to deliver. He'd tried to walk it in, but the dock workers had barred his way. "All closed down now anyway," he said, in his lilting English. "The guys inside—they have stopped for lunch."

So I got back in my truck and waited. I took my checkbook out of my purse and balanced it. I planned my delivery route for the next day. On a tiny notepad I wrote a sixteen-page letter to a friend. Two hours had passed, and I had been able to inch forward one truck length. I got out and stretched, talked to the other drivers. They told me that the area was very unsafe—that young hoodlums would break into waiting trucks and rob them if the drivers left them. They advised me to keep my truck locked. We talked some more. Christmas was not far off, and one driver, recently arrived from Puerto Rico, told me about the beautiful doll he was planning to buy for his daughter back on the island. I gave him a jar of honey to send along. Then I gave out jars of honey to the rest of the drivers. It was getting cold, and we all stamped our feet to stay warm. We moved our trucks another length and complained about Bloomingdale's computer, about computers in general.

We were all getting hungry. Lunch was over for the men inside the warehouse, but none of us had had ours. The Alabamian knew of a Greek restaurant several blocks away, but everyone agreed that it was unsafe for us to leave our trucks, even though they were locked. The men looked around, and decided that I seemed to be reliable. (There is an advantage to growing old and becoming motherly looking.) Everyone dug into his pockets, we put together a kitty, and I took orders: burgers with various fixings, fries, and coffee in differing degrees of lightness and sweetness. I set off on foot for the Greek restaurant, and found it after a wrong turn or two. The counterman cooked our burgers to order and poured our coffees, and, hugging the warm sacks to me, I walked back, against a cold wind, to the drivers. We spread our feast out on a hood top and ate and talked. We talked trucks—the good points of some, the defects of others. We talked driving, and compared hard places for deliveries. We talked families. They showed me pictures of their babies, and I told them about my son in Boston. Occasionally, we got back into our trucks and inched up in line. We talked jobs and how to get them. We talked about what it is like to come to New York from far places and what those far places are like and what they mean to us.

At seven in the evening, I was finally at the unloading bay. I slid out my cartons of honey, the computer processed them, a dock worker signed my invoice, I drove out and waved to the remaining truckers. It was one of the best days I've ever had in New York.

(March 1988)

NINE

City of
the Mind

In late September 1988, I was driving east on the interstate through Illinois in my three-quarter-ton pickup with the extra heavy rear end, which allows me to haul 5,000 pounds of honey at a time from my bee farm in Missouri to the fancy little stores on the East Coast, where I sell it. I needed a cup of coffee, but there seemed to be too much happening at the first truck stop I exited for, so I drove on to the next one. I asked a truck driver what the trouble had been back there. He, CB-informed, knew the answer. "You know that feller running for president—George Bush?—well, he decided to have a cup of coffee over there. Thought it wouldn't hurt to do some campaigning neither." It turned out Bush had brought a few friends—Illinois Governor James Thompson, the usual Secret Service men, and a full spate of country singers—Loretta Lynn, Crystal Gayle, and Peggy Sue. Bush and Thompson had bellied up to the counter, ordered taco salad and chili. The singers sang. And Bush left a fifty-dollar tip.

Truck stops may have been franchised into brightness, showplaces of the wonderful ways to make plastic look like something else, but they still retain a certain demotic appeal to those people around a presidential candidate who plan appearances, and for a Republican the reception was guaranteed to be friendly. In a straw vote taken among truckers stopping at the chain where Bush's men had planned to visit (Unocal, the biggest truck-stop chain in the country), he had received a 49 percent rating over his opponent's 31 percent. And truck-stop owners, businessmen all, have Republican tendencies. The trade and lobbying association that looks after the needs of the $23 billion industry, the National Association of Truckstop Owners, NATSO, based in Alexandria, Virginia, was headed up for seven years by Ronald L. Ziegler. The current president is another Nixon staffer, W. Dewey Clower.

The new edition of the *National Truckstop Directory* has more than 2,700 listings, and over the past fifteen years of trucking honey to market, I've hung out at many of them. When I first began driving my routes I never had enough money to pay for a motel, so I'd pull into a highway rest stop, lock my truck doors, unroll my sleeping bag on the front seat, and sleep there. Then a friend of mine, a trucker, told me about staying in just such a rest stop and having his wallet stolen at knife point by a woman to whom he had opened the door one night when he wanted some companionship. He stays at truck stops now, ones that are brightly lighted and usually patroled by security guards. I do, too. They also, blessedly, have coffee available the moment I wake up, for their restaurants are open twenty-four hours a day. In recent years there have been a lot of changes in truck stops, so this past spring I spent a month traveling across the country to document some of them. Here are pictures from my slide show.

Click. I have, over there in back of the travel store, just bathed in the shower room and now I am sitting in a mauve booth. I'm not really thinking about it, but I have a subliminal understanding that things are not as they seem. There is near-quarry tile on the floor, subdued re-cessed ceiling lights with pretty almost-glass hanging lamps spotlighting each booth. Enlarged photos of 18-wheelers, the big tractor-trailer rigs, screen off the drivers-only section where I am sitting. Color-coordinated silk flowers in plastic baskets that hint at straw decorate each booth. The toe-tapping background music is almost-but-not-quite country. Every-thing is inoffensive, clean, vanilla. The waitresses look uncommonly wholesome in their neat uniforms. I've made a fine lunch from the salad bar and the waitress clears away my dishes while I use the in-booth telephone. At the conclusion of the conversation I will send some copy from the fax machine out in the lobby to the editor to whom I am talking. I am in what the folks at NATSO call a "third-generation" truck stop.

Click. I'm in a second-generation truck stop. It is a bit claustrophobic. The walls are covered in dark wood-grain paneling. I'm sitting at an orange plastic table. The air is blue with smoke. Someone has put a quarter in the jukebox and a voice wails: I told her I'd miss her/As she walked out the door. The menu has line drawings of trucks on it. It runs to open-faced, hot-roast-beef sandwiches and chicken-fried steak. It does also offer a "lite meal"—beef patty with cottage cheese and canned peaches, but Jane Brody probably would not be pleased. Pies are re-flected and multiplied in a revolving, mirror-backed display case in the center of the room. The cream pies have spectacular loft and I know from experience that if I order one the white stuff on top will taste like a combination of marshmallow fluff and the insulation builders blow in between walls. There is a bank of telephones near the cash register, where a woman is settling a driver's fuel bill, and truckers, logbooks in hand, are using them to call their dispatchers. There is a store beyond the cash register that sells things truckers need.

Click. I am in a truck stop that has a gravel parking lot big enough for a couple of tractor-trailer rigs to pull into. The air inside is layered with blue smoke, undisturbed by the ceiling fan, which seems to have given up in despair. The pink-sweatered waitress looks tired, has circles under her eyes. A cook presides over a deep-fat fryer and grill. In the Ladies' Room there is a Love Drops machine. For two quarters I am invited to buy a packet of Love Drops: "Now for those Erotic Body Areas. Each sensuous tasty Drop Stimulates, Arouses, Adds a Tingle of Pure Pleasure. Mouthwatering Flavors. Hot Fudge. Piña Colada. Wild Strawberry. Coconut Cream." Outside, beyond the diesel and gasoline pumps, there is a pay telephone shielded from the weather by a hood. No one is using it. First-generation truck stop. But wait, there is more.

Click. Here is a 1940 movie, *They Drive by Night,* which anyone can rent for their VCR just like I did. Humphrey Bogart is in it, but not as a star. He merely supports George Raft, Ida Lupino, and Ann Sheridan. Bogart and Raft, a pair of truckers, tired beyond belief, stop in at Barney's Roadside Restaurant where all the truckers go for coffee. Raft banters with Sheridan, the waitress.

"Gimme a cup of coffee."

"Anything else?"

"Yeah, what else you got that ain't poisonous?"

"I don't know. I never eat here."

After that (P.S., he gets the girl, but not before Ida Lupino throws a splendid mad scene) Raft *borrows* the telephone from behind the counter after assuring Barney that he will reverse the charges.

The trucks that Bogart and Raft and their friends were driving were small by today's standard and didn't need the space or diesel fuel that present ones do. Forrest Baker, of Baker's Transportation Research and Marketing, consultant to the truck-stop industry and historian of it, says that the old "gas pots" didn't completely disappear until the 1960s. He also says that the words "truck stop" were first used by Richfield Oil when it built its West Coast chain in the 1950s. Pure Oil, the Southern predecessor of Union 76, now Unocal, shares the credit for starting what became today's truck stop by building twenty-four-hour-a-day facilities without locks, so that they had to be staffed every day of the year, around the clock. Baker tells the story of Orrin Jarrell, who opened what is now the Texaco Virginia Travel Plaza at Exit 40 off I-95 back in the 1950s. Jarrell didn't have enough money to hire a night staff so he slept on the floor with his feet against the door. When a customer came, the push on the door would awaken him.

Bigger trucks and the interstate highway system spurred the truck-stop industry. When I first began writing about truck stops in 1985, I said that "there is a city of the mind that stretches from coast to coast, from border to border. Its cross streets are the interstate highways, and food, comfort, companionship are served up in its buildings, the truck stops near the exits. Its citizens . . . are the truckers and waitresses at the stops." Today that city of the mind provides nearly everything that those less mobile find in their own more circumscribed cities and the City of the Mind has two million inhabitants (NATSO estimates that there are 1.8 million truckers and that each truck stop has, on the average, a hundred employees). I made it a rule during my month of travel to stop nowhere but truck stops, and found myself a resident of that city of two million.

The first stop I made was at the Mountain Gate Plaza, an Exxon truck stop, just off Route 15 near Thurmont, Maryland. It spills over the road from one side to the other, with its truck parking lots, gift stores, service garage, bakery, deli, and restaurant. Inside the FAMILY RESTAU-RANT (writ large in mustard-yellow letters on the mansard roof) the decor runs to tan and brown. The waitresses and bus boys smile without cease. There are American flags, pictures of Jesus, and religious plaques in the gift shop. There are stacks of free religious pamphlets and tapes scattered throughout. The menu says "God Bless You" and advises the self-serve buffet. Over the latter a sign admonishes TAKE ALL YOU WANT. EAT ALL YOU TAKE. I felt I must mind my p's and q's. I asked the waitress if the truck stop is connected with a church. She lowered her eyes, smiled even more, and said, "Oh, no. It's a Christian truck stop, but we're nondenominational." If the Mountain Gate is exultant in its fundamentalism, it is only a bit more so than many other truck stops, for there is a down-home Christianity in truck stops across the nation. There are very few that do not have a pile of *Wheels Alive,* a newspaper published by the Association of Christian Truckers ("Reaching the Asphalt Jungles of the Nation") or *Highway Evangelist,* published by Transport for Christ International ("Christ in the World of Trucking"). That first night I stayed at a truck stop outside Carlisle, Pennsylvania, where Chaplain Jack was available twice a week for counseling. I saw a number of chapels at truck stops throughout the country, some fixed (the trailer trimmed up with white plastic siding, the TRANSPORT FOR CHRIST JESUS SAVES, east of Oklahoma City, for instance) or mobile (the Mack truck with trailer emblazoned JESUS FOR TRUCKING Mobile Chapel out on the interstates).

The Amoco All American Auto and Truck Plaza where I spent the first night is a big, serious truck stop. It is at the intersection of a major north-south interstate (I-81) and the Pennsylvania Turnpike (I-76). The woman at the cash register told me that the complex—restaurant, service center, parking lot, and motel—covers about fifty acres. According to one industry authority, Kent Hedman, manager of Truckstops of America, it can cost up to $100,000 per acre to provide paved, lighted parking, and about thirty trucks can park on each acre. This requires a high return on space if a truck stop is to stay profitable. According to an industry analysis, twenty years ago a truck stop could stay in business if it pumped 35,000 to 40,000 gallons of fuel a month. Today profit margins are lower, and they must pump 250,000 gallons just to get by. A few of the bigger stops now pump more than 1.5 million gallons a month, trying to capture their share of the 10 billion gallons of fuel truckers buy from truck stops each year. The scramble for the market is what has pushed truck stops into expanding services to extract more dollars from each trucker when he fuels up, and to attract other travelers in addition to professional drivers. A good restaurant can generate up to 15 cents in food sales for each gallon of gasoline sold. Fuel and related services for truckers are still the biggest part of a truck stop's business, but food and consumer sales to those truckers refer to with just a tinge of contempt as "four-wheelers" are getting bigger all the time.

The Carlisle All American is a notable place in zoological circles, too. It is the only truck stop designated as an official crow roost by the American Crow Society. At 5:30 P.M. on the day I stopped there, both truckers and crows were circling in. The trucks were beginning to fill the big parking lot and the crows were settling into the trees at the edge of it. The sky was soon black with crows, wheeling in from all points. They jabbered with one another as they found roosts, occasionally boiled up from one tree, resettled into another, gossiped. The truckers were doing approximately the same down on the ground. The crows ignored the truckers and the truckers returned the disregard. I was interested in both.

Inside, in the restaurant where I had dinner after the crows were tucked in for the night, tables and booths were packed with truckers. Although there was a salad bar, the menu ran to traditional heavy food. It included a long list of vegetables: french-fried zucchini, french-fried onion rings, french-fried cauliflower, french-fried mushrooms, corn fritters. "A study by an industrial medicine group . . . showed that over 80% of truck drivers surveyed had gained weight since they started trucking. The culprit: stress, boredom, eating on the road, low activity level and sporadic eating schedules," reported one professional drivers' magazine.

At a nearby booth a trucker with a build like Laughing Buddha addressed his mashed potatoes and gravy with a Buddhalike air of quiet happiness. His belly nestled in a bright red T-shirt. He had long hair and a beard. His companion driver, a woman, was tucking into her food, too, but pausing now and again, with a dreamy look in her eyes, to croon "boop . . . boop . . . a . . . boop" to the country-music beat which was all that could be heard over the clatter of silverware and dishes and coffee-stimulated talk. I eavesdropped shamelessly on the conversation of a pair of truckers at the booth in front of me. A driver with a handlebar mustache and a Tennessee accent was complaining to the one whose back was to me about troopers hassling truckers at the western state line of Maryland, where the speed limit drops to the East Coast fifty-five. ". . . Two marked cars and one plain brown wrapper. Hell, they was arrestin' guys. Goddam' handcuffs." The conversation rolled on to radar detectors, lawyers. Said Tennessee, "I got two goddam' lawyers, one at home and one in upstate New York and I'm still not makin' any money."

After dinner I wandered into the travel store to buy postcards and then went searching for the mailbox up on the second floor, where the showers, video-game room, and TV are. It was hot and stuffy there, packed with men passing the time. I spotted the UPS drop, found the mailbox. Outside in the cool air the crows were quiet. Many of the truckers were also asleep in beds in the back of their cabs.

In preparation for my trip I had sent fifteen dollars to Unocal. In return I received a professional driver's card, a keen belt buckle and key chain with lions' heads on them, a patch for my jacket, a decal, and a lifetime subscription to *Road King* magazine, a quarterly full of news about trucking, truck stops, gossip (a lot of marriages take place in truck stops) and jokes. Sample joke:

At a driving rally, the 74 year old owner of a trucking company was in the process of parking his rig near a stone wall. A young guy in a red sports car darted into the space ahead of him. The young fellow got out of his car and said "That's what it's like to be 18 and spry."

The trucker backed up his rig and, at full speed, hit the sports car, jamming it into a heap against the wall. He climbed out of the truck and said, "That's what it's like to be old and rich." —Les Bostic, Decatur, Georgia

I also received in my membership packet a stack of truckerbucks worth fifteen dollars. Many of my truckerbucks were for things like partial payment on a lube job for my 18-wheeler, but some of them could be spent at any Unocal Travel Store. They were burning a hole in my pocket, so the next day I stopped at New Stanton West Unocal Auto/ Truck Plaza at Exit 23, near Smithton on the Pennsylvania Turnpike. I gassed up and went into the travel store, where I did just what they wanted. I spent more than I had in truckerbucks. I bought an atlas showing truck routes and other useful information, a pair of wonderful ventilated sunglasses, and a trucker's cap. All of my life I have wanted a cap that said MACK on it. It would have been more loyal, I suppose, to have bought one that said FORD—that is what my three-quarter-ton truck is—but the Ford one was not beautiful and the Mack is: gorgeous royal blue, with a Mack truck bulldog standing tough. He is set off by scrolls of gold leaf. I put it on, and as I walked through the parking lot the driver of a big Navistar waved.

Down the road, at the Amoco American Truckstop at exit 12B, I stopped for lunch. I slouched into the professional drivers' section still wearing my cap. A typical truckdriver wears cowboy boots, a hand-tooled leather belt and . . . always . . . inside and out . . . his cap. It is the way most men would dress, I bet, if they didn't have to go to an office. Several drivers nodded. I reached for the in-booth telephone and placed a call to my dispatcher . . . um . . . my husband. While I was talking, the waitress moved in with coffee. She raised an eyebrow. I nodded. She poured. After I'd finished my call I grabbed a menu and she returned. Her eyes were sad but she was hustling tips and had her quip ready. "Yer time's up." I ordered. Gigantic, gaudy, plastic-wrapped plush bunnies crouched above the salad bar waiting to be taken home as Easter presents by drivers. The jukebox played Willie Nelson: "Forgivin' you was easy. Forgettin' takes a longer time. . . ." I ate. I asked the waitress for my check. "Sure, nobody else wanted it."

At the West Virginia state line, I punched in the cruise control at sixty-five and rolled west. I lived out of truck stops. I found truck stops that had good food, bad food; truck stops that had shoeshine stands; truck stops with Laundromats, movie rentals, in-booth coin-op TV, lottery tickets, barbershops, and beauty parlors. The Indy West Unocal, exit 59 off I-70, offers, among other things, haircut ($7), beard trim ($5), cut and perm ($30), ear piercing ($5). I found a truck stop with a knife-and scissor-sharpening stand, one with a pawnshop. What do truckers pawn? An antique sequined-and-beaded purse cost $45, a cloisonné napkin ring was $24, a "germany" screwdriver $9. I found a truck stop with a legitimate massage clinic and one that had a wake-up service for truckers sleeping in their rigs. I found truck stops that were entire shopping malls. I found horoscope, sex-potential, and biorhythm machines (the last always showed me as "moribund"). I heard reports of truck stops with resident dentists, chiropractors, hot tubs, swimming pools, weight and exercise rooms. And truckers. I saw truckers everywhere. I saw truckers with glazed eyes sitting watching TV in rooms with bad air. Truckers come labeled. Their caps say BAMA TRUCKS, LITTLEFIELD LIGHTNING, MY NAME IS HENRY. Their jackets say KEN BURCH TRUCKING, BULLPEN, KEY WAY, ROLL ON ALABAMA. Their T-shirts say ROAD REBEL, SAYRE'S TRUCK OASIS, WILD AND FREE. Truckers are guys shut up in truck cabs most of the day, driving schedules that are, sometimes, impossible to meet legally. At truck stops they talk garrulously. They talk routes, cops, mechanical problems. I watched three women truckers in a booth in a truckstop in Amarillo. They were wearing PRIME, INC. caps. Two of them were cooperatively untangling a coiled piece of wire. The third was working on a trucker's log. They all were pale, looked serious, preoccupied.

"WnRooOAARrRRthRmmmOOOAARrrrulRny?" a truck driver in a PRO AM cap asked me outside the door of a truck stop as a big rig roared by.

"What?" I cupped my hand behind my ear.

"Want some company?" he repeated.

"No, not really."

He blushed furiously and fled.

I began to think like a trucker. I needed a post office one day when I was in the West, but, because it was Sunday, the one at the Tucson Truck Terminal was closed. "Oh, well," I thought, "there's that one at the Petro Truckstop outside of Joplin. I'll use it instead." That's Joplin, Missouri, more than a thousand miles away. I had become a citizen of the City of the Mind.

You don't have to be a citizen to use truck-stop facilities. Here is how you take a shower at a truck stop if you haven't bought a lot of fuel (usually fifty gallons or more will get you a free one). You hand over ten dollars to the cashier in the travel store and she gives you a big fluffy towel, a bar of soap, and a numbered key. She nods in the direction of the shower room, which is a long corridor with locked rooms facing out on to it. Your key will unlock one of those numbered doors. Inside there will be a sink, a toilet, a big shower, and a bench. The room will be tiled and clean. After you have showered, you take your towel and key back to the cashier and she returns five dollars to you.

When I got to the Joplin Petro with its post office, exit 4 off I-44, I talked to the store manager, Richard Leavens. He is a stocky, cheerful young man with glasses. He took me on a tour of the truck stop, which is vibrant, brightly colored, gleaming. He showed me the post office, shower room, Laundromat, Western Union and fax machines. The travel store twinkles with heaps of chrome exhaust pipes and other truck accessories. "We got more chrome in here than anywhere else," Leavens said proudly. I believe him. The TV room had enough chairs to make a movie theater and it had been filled over the weekend, when eleven inches of snow fell in a late spring storm, stranding the truckers. Leavens said the lot was filled. Two hundred trucks had squeezed into the twenty-eight acres of parking. Leavens said that, second to airports, more telephone calls are placed in truck stops than anywhere else, and there were, in addition to the in-booth phones in the restaurant, banks of telephones near the shoeshine stand, most of them in use as we talked. Out in the parking lot he waved his hand at the 100,000-gallon water-storage tank, 2-million-gallon fuel-storage area, the warehouse-sized storeroom. "Sure are a lot of truck stops being built," he said. "I wonder if there are *too* many. I don't know whether I like these big chains taking over everything. I'd like to run my own small business, but it's more efficient this way." Roger King of NATSO had told me that it now takes $5 to $7 million in capital to start a truck stop, a site that is at least forty acres, and some in-depth traffic studies. It is hard for a young man like Leavens to come up with a package like that. Petro or Amoco or Texaco or Unocal can. According to King, even some of the old-established, individually owned truck stops, which still account for half of those in business, are affiliating with the chains.

Leavens said that the chains work hard to attract tourists to what Petro calls "Stopping Centers." But the preeminence of the professional truck driver had been made clear to me one night early in my trip when I had stopped to fuel up. I had used the self-service pump and gone inside to pay the cashier. She started to take my money, then turned to take care of another trucker, who was billing one of the intermediate credit services that handles truck fleet accounts. His bill was $314. Mine was $13.50. It was obvious why I should be kept waiting.

East of Gallup I exited from I-40 at No. 39 to visit the Giant Travel Center, a truck stop which had been advertising itself with the avidity of a Harrald's Club for a hundred miles. I was struck by the kinship between truck stops and farmers' roadside stands. Just as farmers peddle their produce alongside the road, so do petroleum companies peddle theirs at truck stops. Nowhere is that more apparent than at the Giant. It takes up 880 acres, 745 of which are the hillside Giant refinery, a big industrial facility of pipes and purpose. Down below is the travel center, where gasoline and diesel fuel from the refinery are sold. The truck stop is a 40,000-square-foot shopping mall. Inside there are restaurants and, yes, boutiques. "Gotcha Covered" is a clothing store. "Sweet Temptations" a candy shop. There is also a TV lounge with a fireplace, laundry service for those who don't want to use the Laundromat, the usual FedEx, photocopy rooms, shoeshine stand, showers, and, in addition, a movie theater that shows twelve first-run movies serially, with ten-minute breaks in between. I have a rule about pie: never order pie in a restaurant within one mile of an interstate highway. But the big restaurant at Giant had its own bakery, so I decided to test my rule and ordered apple pie. It had a thick, heavy crust and a jellylike filling with a few tasteless apples floating in it. There is no need to change my rule. Petroleum companies should not make pies.

I turned south and truck stopped my way down to Tucson, where, early on a Sunday morning I had my coffee at the Triple T (as it is called by those who have gone to it over the years). The Exxon Tucson Truck Terminal, one of the oldest truck stops in the country still in business, is at Exit 268 off I-10 east of Tucson. The Terminal was built in the mid sixties by Ira Morris, who is still president although he does not actively manage it any longer. Morris, according to Forrest Baker, understood that "basically, truckers are just lonely guys. So Ira kept a cat . . . well, maybe it was several cats, because their life spans weren't so long . . . and he had a rocking chair there, too, and the guys would come in and sit in the rocking chair and pet the cat and the cat would purr and be as affectionate as could be and it was real homey. But Ira had trained that cat so no one could take it out the front door. If he tried, the cat would scratch and fight and wouldn't go. No one knew how he did it."

The cat and the rocking chair were nowhere to be seen the Sunday morning I was there, but the lonely guys were. They were in no rush to go and were staring off into space, smoking, drinking coffee, and eating too much breakfast: $5.50 bought the special—two thick strips of bacon, a slice of ham, two extra-large eggs, home fries, buttermilk biscuits with gravy.

One morning on the way back home a lonely guy who was a woman struck up a conversation with me at the Truckstops of America at Exit 273 off I-10, just past Santa Rosa, New Mexico. (TA, as the chain is known, prints interesting facts below its menu special. Some are: TA serves 1 million pounds of french fries a year, TA waitresses pour more than 20 million cups of coffee each year.) The woman and I were both sitting in the No Smoking section. She was waiting for her husband, who is also a driver, to come back from the shower. They had slept the night in their cab in the TA lot. She had short, curly, sandy-colored hair. She was plump, round-faced, hungry for talk. She had been driving with her husband ever since their children were grown. They lived in Wisconsin and regularly hauled school supplies between there and California. When her husband was working by himself he used to drive on the East Coast, where the routes were hard and stressful. He'd be home often, but when he got there he was tired and tense. He switched to the West, where the driving was easier, but he was home less often. "I cried for a solid month when he changed, because he kept missing family events. I couldn't understand about the big distances out here. I'd say, 'Honey, can't you just press the pedal to the metal and hurry home?' He couldn't, and now that I drive with him I can see why. When I started, my husband went to his boss and said 'Now she's not gonna work like a man. We're gonna have six hours of sleep every night, six hours in a truck stop, asleep in our bunk. No more than fourteen or fifteen hours on the job,' and his boss said that sounded reasonable." Her husband returned, clean and freshly shaved, and nodded to me. They turned their attention to the menu. The wife exclaimed over the French toast, which she remembered having there before and ordered it, asking the waitress to make sure it had plenty of powdered sugar, extra powdered sugar.

I drove on.

Recent figures show that only a little more than 4 percent of professional truck drivers are women. Most of those drive with a husband or other male partner. Very few drive solo. Truck stops used to have a Men Only sort of aspect to them, but today there are women's restrooms in the professional drivers' sections and showers and laundry facilities are open to all. The travel stores stock hair curlers and cosmetics as well as shaving cream. Still, women are such a tiny minority that when I would stand at the doorway of a darkened TV room, wander into the lounge or game room late at night, I was conscious of being female, an outsider. For many years women in truck stops were of two sorts—waitresses or prostitutes. And when women began driving they were suspect. An article in a 1985 issue of *Road King* lays out the problem:

The most degrading experience of all for women truckers is the fact they are asked to leave parking areas, restaurants, and truck stops because they are (1) women and (2) alone. It is presumed that because they are alone they must be soliciting. Admittedly, prostitutes are a big problem for some truck stops. The majority of male truck drivers are decent, hardworking family men. . . . They need their sleep. They don't want to be disturbed at all hours of the night by knocks on the door of their cab.

That was four years ago, and truck stops have tackled the problem of what are called "lot lizards" by fencing off the truck parking area and barring admission to it for pickups and cars. Most have signs that say NO SOLICITING ON TRUCKSTOP PROPERTY or words to that effect. Some sting operations have been set up and some lots are patrolled by security guards. But regulating the world's oldest profession is as difficult in the City of the Mind as it is in any other city. And CBs make it easy to make connections. A friend of mine teaches special education in a school in southern Missouri, and she told me about an emotionally damaged

eleven-year-old boy who is one of her students. His mother is a prostitute who works a truck stop I know well. With her son on the seat beside
her she drives her pickup to a roadside park each night and, using her
CB, offers herself up to truck drivers as they roll by. When she has lined
up a john, she drives over to the truck stop. The trucker usually buys
the little boy a Royal Crown, which he drinks in a booth inside the truck
stop while his mother repairs to the bunk in the trucker's rig. My friend
said the little boy came to school recently talking about the nice trucker
who had showed him how to check the tires on his rig by kicking them,
and who had bought him a whole piece of pie because he hadn't had any
supper. He was happy, too, because his mother had given him his own
CB handle—Sweet Betsy. He had giggled and confided that the truckers
think he is a girl when he talks to them. My friend is afraid the little boy
is being trained for a specialty trade.

The CB also makes it easier to make connections to buy drugs.
Truck-stop drug sales are much discussed in all the current trucker
magazines. Of course there are drugs and then there are drugs. In
hearings before the U.S. Senate Commerce Committee, a preliminary
study was cited indicating that 30 percent of truckers used drugs, but 11
percent of that was stimulants, some of it prescription medicine, perhaps
legal, perhaps not, for the study did not differentiate. Staying alert on
long drives, I can testify, is a problem, and according to published
reports, many of the parking-lot/truck-stop drug sales are uppers, on
which truckers may be throwing away their money, believing them to
be strong prescription drugs when laboratory tests show they are only
the equivalent of a cup of coffee.

When I got back to the East Coast I invited my husband out for a
trucker's date. I'd read that the Texaco Truckers' Inn at Exit 41 off I-95
south of Baltimore had a hot tub. It doesn't (the lady at the desk said a
sister truck stop in Baltimore *does*, however) and its swimming pool was
closed for the season. What the Truckers' Inn does have, however, is live

entertainment every night. So we had dinner of steak and fries (my husband unwisely also ordered coconut-cream pie) and then we went downstairs to the Eighteen-Wheeler Lounge. There was a two-dollar cover charge to go into the low-ceilinged, L-shaped room. There were two TV sets in operation down at one end, a bar with a sign over it reading ON DUTY DRIVERS PLEASE DO NOT ASK US TO SERVE YOU ALCOHOLIC BEVERAGES. Balloons and streamers decorated the room. Smoke lay stratified in the air. When we came in, the band (Tall in the Saddle—drums, pedal steel guitar, two electric guitars, and a violin with a pickup) were playing Chubby Checkers, "The Twist." There was a crowd of at least a hundred truckers and trucker groupies, most of them dancing. We slung our jackets over chairs at a vacant table and elbowed our way out onto the dance floor. My husband was wearing a bad, bad black T-shirt I had bought him, with a shimmering 3-D truck bursting out of the legend TRUCKERS MAKE AMERICA GREAT and a cap he had just bought in the travel store that said COAST TO COAST. I was wearing my MACK cap and a matching T-shirt that said ROAD REBEL. The crowd was friendly, relaxed. There were some pitchers of beer sitting on the tables but no one was loud or drunk or rowdy. Some of the groupies started out on the dance floor with each other, but partners shifted during the rock-and-roll numbers. CAT TRACTOR moved opposite me, grinning with great good humor. The band started playing country and western, and two fat women, one without shoes, danced with a tiny little man. A girl with a very short skirt and pretty, long, black-stockinged legs stomped tirelessly in her high-heeled red shoes with bows at the back. At the beginning of a slow number, NORTH AMERICAN VAN LINES led out a dignified, conservatively dressed teenager and held her delicately, dancing with enough distance between them to please the chaperones at my 1950s high school. Other couples clutched, petted, hugged passionately, kissed wetly. The stars of the evening, to me at least, were the tableful of handsome, young, dark-eyed truckers speaking in Spanish. They were wearing the usual trucker garb, but when they came out on the dance floor I noticed that one of them had silver toes and heels on his cowboy boots. They were wonderful, sexy, skilled dancers. I yearned to have silver toes ask me to dance. He didn't. I'm older by at least a quarter of a century and only a sometime resident of his city.

(November 1989)

Tout Confort and Chocolate

My husband likes to go places he's been before and I like to go places new to me, so when we began discussing a late summer holiday I said we could compromise and go someplace where *neither* of us had ever been. And then, before he could examine that compromise too closely, I began talking about canoeing in the boundary waters. The term "boundary waters" refers to the water and land lying astraddle the Minnesota–Ontario border. It includes, but is not encompassed by, on the American side, the Boundary Waters Canoe Area, and, on the Canadian, Quetico Provincial Park.

All of my life I've been hearing about the boundary waters from friends who enjoy what I like doing—poking around outdoors in the company of wild things. It was more than thirty-five years ago that I first understood that I was going to spend a good deal of time being uncomfortable in places that were hard to get to in order to indulge myself in this liking. I was with some other undergraduates and we were accompanying a graduate researcher who was collecting sea plankton off the coast of North Carolina. There were no motels or places to eat nearby and the weather was hot. The land running down to the ocean grew prickly plants that were a splendid habitat for ticks and mosquitoes. We slept on the beach and cooked food we had carried in. We had a fine time. We were camping, although none of us thought of it that way.

I have never quite understood the penchant for camping for its own sake, eating sooty food and sleeping on the ground, making oneself deliberately uncomfortable with the idea that it builds character in some undefined way, but because they don't build Holiday Inns in the kinds of places I go to do the things I like, I have often been too cold or too hot, tired and improperly fed doing what most people call camping.

Not long ago I married a man who shares some of my interests in the outdoors but who has quite a different approach to it. German-born, European in manner, Arne believes in what the French call *tout confort*. "Wouldn't you take a little miso soup, darling?" he asks, as he fashions a fragment of tinfoil into a cookpot and extracts a soup packet from a pocket I had never known he had. He always has a pair of dry socks and a Band-Aid for blisters. In a canoe he steadily hands out convenience items from plastic bags—when the sun comes out a dab of suntan lotion, when the wind comes up a well-folded parka. In short, now that the two of us are old enough to merit a senior citizen's discount at Denny's, we approach camping entirely differently. I love it.

Eventually my compromise worked out, and in midsummer we drove in my truck from my farm in Missouri to explore the boundary waters, a place that on the map appears to have more water than land. The thousands of lakes there have been cut out by volcanoes and glaciers. The land was so scoured and rearranged by those forces that the rock exposed is some of the oldest that can be seen on the planet—some of it three billion years old.

The area, strictly speaking, has been too severely altered by logging and mining to be true wilderness, although by slogging over particularly difficult terrain to places such as McNiece Lake in Quetico Provincial Park, virgin pines can be found. But native trees, pines, spruce, cedar, fir, and birch, have grown back after the logging, and in the park areas logging has been banned on both sides of the border since the 1970s.

Motorboats are forbidden in Quetico and on many of the lakes in the Boundary Waters Canoe Area, too. Both parks have a ban on bottles and disposable containers. Food and beverages must be repacked into containers that will be carried back out or that can be burned. Camping is controlled through a permit system more restrictively on the Canadian side of the border, yet even so, hundreds of thousands of people each year visit the area, drawn by its beauty, its reputation for fishing, and something else—something vaguer, an amalgam of its history, Indians, traders, trappers, the association with difficult portages, big animals, early morning mists, the writings of Aldo Leopold and Sigurd F. Olson, all amounting to what one local outfitter inventively calls "The Aura of Mystique."

Local outfitters have made the lakes easily accessible. They can arrange fly-in fishing trips to remote lakes, transport canoes by motor launch to less-traveled ones, supply all camping gear down to the last first-aid kit, provide a steak dinner as a send-off, obtain needed permits and maps, pack up freeze-dried turkey tetrazzini, and refer to you all the while as voyageur. Or they will simply rent you a canoe. Or provide any amount of service in between.

A telephone call or a letter to the chambers of commerce in either Ely or Grand Marais, Minn., two of the most popular starting points for Americans, will fill your mailbox with fliers from outfitters for months to come and give you an idea of the range of prices and services available. Alternatively, a day spent in either town taking advantage of the outfitters' knowledge and zeal will prepare any newcomer for what we learned was called a quality wilderness experience.

But Arne and I are anarchists at heart and we were slightly put off by the lavishness of the outfitters and the rules made necessary by so many other voyageurs within the parks. We were advised to obtain park permits a month in advance during peak usage (post-blackfly season, July and August), to stop paddling by 2:00 P.M. in order to get an authorized campsite, and to keep our dog, Tazzie, who never strays more than ten feet, on a leash on all portages. Several friends who have been going to the north woods all their lives told us that the Boundary Waters had so wonderfully focused and concentrated visitors that we could "do the boundary waters without doing the Boundary Waters," so we left Grand Marais and headed north to Ontario on U.S. 61. We crossed the border with rabies vaccination certificate in hand for Tazzie.

Just west of Thunder Bay, Ontario, we stopped at a Shell station to buy fishing and camping permits, all we would need outside park boundaries, and ate lunch in the adjacent café. On Highway 11 we found lodging on the edge of a clear, cold lake at Birch Point Resort. We rented a small but comfortable cabin with a stove and refrigerator. To Arne's delight he discovered a sauna at the lake's edge—*tout confort.* Down the highway we found Canadian Quetico Outfitters run by Roger Thew, a sometime gold prospector with his hair tied back in a ponytail. He rented us a canoe, a lightweight Grumann. That was all we needed, for we had our own camping gear and had stocked up on lightweight food in a city grocery store in Missouri before we left on our trip. Had we needed them, however, outfitters in Atikokan, on Highway 11, near the entrance to Quetico, could have provided all supplies and services.

There is a peculiarity to time in this area that puts one in a vacation mood. Technically this part of Ontario is in the central time zone. However, most residents do their serious shopping in Thunder Bay, which is in the eastern time zone, and so for the sake of convenience they usually keep their clocks on Thunder Bay time. Usually, but not always. So there is a vagueness about time and any appointment has a two-hour leeway. Nice.

We bought some maps and by studying them and taking the local advice, freely given, we worked out several expeditions. We planned each one around a portage. Lakes portaged into, of course, are inaccessible to motorboats and we wanted to keep away from their noise and wakes, which often jostle a canoe in an inconsiderate way. A rule about portages: the longer and harder they are, the fewer people will make them.

Our first portage was a boggy half-mile wallow in which we could float our canoe on the ooze as often as carry it and we slogged through the black mucky stuff up to our calves. Arne's canoe-carrying technique is unique. He scorns the usual canoe yoke that balances an overturned canoe on the bearer's shoulders. Instead, before we had left Missouri, he cut himself a slim but strong oak branch longer than the canoe is wide, and lashed it across the top of his backpack. He carried the canoe balanced on that. This served to transfer the weight of the canoe to his hips, where the pack was braced and where it was more comfortable. I carried the rest of our gear in my backpack. At the end of the portage we were hot and wet, but Arne dried us out and produced a packet of lemonade mix which he stirred into a plastic container of water.

After that portage we saw no other human beings and only an occasional sign of one at flat spots along banks where someone had left a fire circle of stones and a stash of dry wood. This is awe-inspiring country. It invites respect and tidiness, and we saw no litter anywhere. We were on the kinds of lakes that are the best for canoeing—long and narrow, not wide enough for winds to build up and make paddling difficult. The weather was fine. The morning mists were properly spectral. It was sunny in the daytime and the water sparkled. Ontario's famous mosquitoes were mostly past their population peak. Birch gleamed white through the fir and cedar at the water's edge.

The nights were cold enough to make snuggling into down sleeping bags a pleasure and we fell asleep to the call of loons who had accompanied us during our daytime paddling beset by the curiosity that affects them when they seldom see humans. We could readily see the shores from the canoe while we were on the water, and we saw red fox and moose. I was delighted to learn that the white-throated sparrow, which we Americans usually characterize as calling "Old Sam Peabody Peabody Peabody," north of the border sings "Oh Poor Canada Canada Canada." It does indeed. The common woodland birds were everywhere—brown creepers, red-eyed vireos, several sorts of jays. I did not see a three-toed woodpecker, although I looked hard for that rarity. It was impossible to miss the evening grosbeaks, those handsome gregarious birds with their sturdy beaks and buttery yellow plumage.

There are black bears that, at night, make it necessary to tie up food packs high in the trees, but we never saw any, possibly because we had Tazzie along. I was grateful that she had a painful lesson far behind her and knew enough to avoid porcupines, another resident of these woods. She is equally wary of skunks, which she knows from Missouri. At night she stayed close and in the daytime resigned herself to curling up in the canoe between us except when a chipmunk or squirrel chittered what must have amounted to dog insults. Then she would jump up and peer at the shore. The water was calm, but we learned to make instant adjustments as she shifted her attention (and thereby her weight) to port or starboard squirrel.

In between our outings we returned to Birch Point for showers, sauna, the kitchenette, and a soft bed. One afternoon we walked down the railroad tracks to Kashabowie, a town so small it is blessed with two-digit telephone numbers. (Birch Point is Kashabowie 29). There is one store in town, a general store, presided over by the town's "mayor," Whisky Bill, who started his commercial life as a trader to the Ojibwa Indians. He sat staring out of the window of the store waiting for company that afternoon. He seemed glad to have someone to talk to and advised us on canoe routes, the handling of birch-bark canoes, and told us Indian stories. Walking back I picked a wildflower bouquet for our cabin: pearly everlasting, butter-and-eggs, tansy, and fireweed.

The area around Kashabowie is instructive in a subtle way that official parkland, where logging is forbidden and the illusion of wilderness is created, is not. Outside the park boundaries it is permissible to log to within 300 feet of the lakes. Saw logs are long since gone, but small trees are cut for pulpwood to feed our insatiable hunger for newsprint. Wherever the land has been clear-cut, leaving it stark, ugly, and distressed, the need for the park as a reserve for what the land can be is apparent. Aldo Leopold, who worked as hard as anyone to preserve this area, wrote with clear sight in *The Sand County Almanac* in 1949:

For the first time in the history of the human species, two changes are now impending. One is the exhaustion of wilderness in the more habitable portions of the globe. The other is the worldwide hybridization of cultures through modern transport and industrialization. Neither can be prevented, and perhaps should not be, but the question arises whether by some slight amelioration of the impending changes, certain values can be preserved that would otherwise be lost.

We all know the ponderous and high-minded reasons for these values and for holding on to wild places, but in the end Leopold, again, said it most profoundly and most simply: "We seek contacts with nature because we derive pleasure from them."

It is a pleasure I have sought all my life and, I suppose, I will continue to seek it for the rest of my days. And if the backpack seems heavier and I mind the cold toes more than I used to, well, now I have a partner who helps make that seeking easier, who practices *tout confort*. "You look tired, my love. Wouldn't you care for a bit of chocolate?"

(June 1990)

ELEVEN

Bug Art

An elegantly dressed blond woman was spiritedly holding forth on the Meaning of It All. It was hard to pay attention to what she was saying, because her two long antennae jounced and curtsied as she nodded her head for emphasis. The antennae, which were made of cloth-wrapped wire and ended in yellow cotton balls, were held on her head by a plastic bandeau; they looked like the Deely Bobbers that sprang from the heads of ten-year-olds on the streets of New York a few years ago. The antennaed woman and 499 other St. Louisans who were interested in the finer things had paid fifteen dollars each for the privilege of celebrating the opening of a special kind of art exhibition. They had come together on a mild afternoon late in September at the city's Laumeier Sculpture Park, which boasts work by Richard Serra, Mary Miss, Mark di Suvero, and others, to attend the installation of a show by Garnett Puett, an apisculptor (*apis* is the Latin word for bee), who had, with his bees, been working during the spring and summer on a piece commissioned by Laumeier. The sculpture was done, the honeybees were gone, but Puett was there. Puett, a New Yorker, is point man, as it were, of this particular kind of art today.

A big blue-and-white striped tent had been put up on the lawn in back of the Laumeier gallery. Black and yellow (bee colors) gas-filled balloons were tethered at its corners. Inside, a string band—its members decked out in white shirts, black pants, and yellow sashes—was playing gypsy music. Puett's wife, Whendi, who was the model for the commissioned work, was there, in a black dress, and Puett had given her a yellow rose to wear with it. Tables were piled with food, and there was an open bar. As the noise level rose, only scraps of conversation could be picked up.

"Queen bee left all of a sudden and they called the artist . . ."

"A little weird . . ."

"It *is* art, because it's creating something upon a form."

"Trying to leave the sculpture another month, but the queen bee left . . ."

"It is *not* art. No, not human art. Bee art, maybe. This young man is *exploiting* bees."

In front of the commissioned piece stands a young woman, stunned. The piece, *Apiscaryatid,* is a record of a completed process. It is a life-size naked female figure of beeswax. One foot is held slightly to one side. The arms are held in back, hands clasped. The head is in a relaxed position. The whole stance is easy, natural. The young woman gazing at the figure says, "I came prepared to laugh at this, but I'm moved by its power beyond telling."

Because, as a beekeeper, I spend a portion of my workdays at the edge of entomology, thinking about bugs and trying to figure out what they are up to, friends from more acceptable trades are constantly sending me clippings about insects and telling me funny bug stories. It is their attempt to keep in touch with my entomological half, which they consider quaintly charming but a bit mad.

Not long ago, I realized that in among the piles of clippings reporting bizarre incidents—like one about a man in Florida who pulled out his pistol and shot himself in the leg to kill an (unidentified) bug that was crawling up it—were lots of stories about people committing art with insects. The clippings from art magazines and newspaper art columns indicated that the critics were taking the individual artists seriously— too seriously—but that none had grasped the fact that each show was more than an isolated event. I've discovered a trend, a movement, and I'm going to claim a discoverer's privilege and name it: Bug Art.

There are straight representations. Terry Winters, a New York artist, paints insects on canvas, for instance. Some venture further and use bug parts. In Beijing, Cao Yijian takes cicadas apart and reassembles them as three-dimensional figures. In New York, Richard Boscarino uses whole (though dead) cockroaches to create what he calls still-lifes. In Los Angeles, Kim Abeles has made what she calls a metaphor for rush-hour traffic, in her *Great Periodic Migration*, consisting partly of cicada shells. A Japanese artist, Kazuo Kadonaga, has live silkworms spin cocoons in wooden grids. The worms having been killed, the cocoons, in their frameworks, were displayed early this year in his Los Angeles gallery. Garnett Puett works in cooperation with live honeybees to create his apisculptures. I hear rumors of a man with a pigtail who makes living sculptures with turtles. Someone is doing something with live crayfish. Regretfully, I force myself to ignore vertebrates and crustaceans, to hold the line at insects. But then there is a man with an ant farm he calls art. What is going on?

In his show in February and early March, at the respected Los Angeles gallery Space, Kazuo Kadonaga displayed nearly a hundred pieces of work, created by 100,000 silkworms. He had fashioned wooden grids, some standing alone, some stacked, and had released on them silkworms that had been fed until they were ready to spin cocoons. Silkworms seek protected niches, and these silkworms explored the wooden gridwork until they found spots to suit them. In the beginning,

Kadonaga gave them freedom to wander as they pleased, but they bunched together at the tops of the grids and left the bottom niches unoccupied. So he and his assistant spent forty-eight hours periodically turning the grids while the silkworms roamed, thereby tricking them into behaving as though down were up and so was sideways, and the worms settled into an even, though not uniform, distribution across the grids to spin their cocoons. (Some niches were never taken by any silkworm, some contained two.) This amounts to a practical joke on the silkworms, but it is aesthetically pleasing to the human eye. Silkworms spin threads in an enthusiastic and generous way. Not only did Kadonaga's make fat silken cocoons, the size of slightly shrunk Ping-Pong balls, in his grids but they left light, fluffy thread trails as they crawled to their preferred niches. The completed pieces are a contrast between the precise, geometric wooden forms and the rounded shapes of the cocoons, the whole fuzzed up with trailing silk. After the silkworms finished their cocoons, each piece was heated to kill the worms inside—a process similar to the one followed in sericulture, or silk farming, when the silkworms must be heated and killed, lest they emerge as moths and break the long silk threads before a human being can harvest them.

Kadonaga's gallery displayed all ninety-one of his pieces in one divided space where, crowded together, they looked like a cityscape. It was a witty display—after all, if you are going to ask 100,000 worms to work for you, the total effect is very much to the point—but that aspect of the show slipped by the reviewers, one of whom, Chuck Nicholson, writing in *Artweek* of 21 March 1987, grumbled that the grouping "seriously detracts from the impact of individual pieces." Being an art critic must be a sobering job; at least, none of the current critics seem to be having much fun reviewing Bug Art.

Kadonaga speaks little English and is only sometimes in this country, but Jeri Coates, who is the assistant director of Space, reports that he was born in 1946 in Ishikawa-ken, is tall—nearly six feet—and has long, curly hair. "He has a droll wit," Coates says. "A puckish sense of humor. He is an actor, a natural mimic, who can transform himself before your eyes into someone else."

Today, Kadonaga lives in Tsurugimachi, near the Sea of Japan, where he is known as Kichigai, or the Crazy One, partly because he is an artist in a well-to-do family that is in the lumber business. His father had hoped Kadonaga would join the business, but he'd decided he wanted to become an artist. He began by painting, but realized, he said in a 1984 interview, through an interpreter, that "others painted better." In his father's sawmill he rediscovered wood, which, he said, "brought out my true artist's personality." He began to play with it. "I am not creating beauty but discovering the natural beauty of material," he said in another interview. He sliced wood into thin layers and allowed it to dry and curl. He scored logs and encouraged them to check. He made regular grooves in logs and then whacked them with a samurai sword, and the scored fissures exploded throughout the interior of the logs to emerge in unpredictable jagged lines on the other side. He gathered bamboo, frayed it, bent it, arranged it, and called it art. Handmade paper, a lovely material, diverted him for a while. He had it made in unusual shapes (triangles, strips, oblongs), stacked it wet, and clamped it. As the paper dried, the unclamped portions fluffed up, and he displayed the pieces in a 1983 gallery show. All this was before he got to silkworms. A catalog of his shows from the presilkworm period has been published and contains somewhat precious, dramatic, and seductively gorgeous photographs, which, in effect, become an aspect of his work.

Kadonaga has had shows in Japan as well as in the Netherlands, Mexico, Germany, Sweden, New Zealand, and Australia. "In Japan, they have turned their back on his art, because they don't know what to make of this man," Edward Lau, the director of the Space gallery, says. Lau believes that Kadonaga's work is at once too traditional and too unusual for Japanese buyers. The Japanese, says Lau, have always understood the beauty of the natural materials Kadonaga is using, but Western buyers are just beginning to discover it. The silkworm pieces, which, at least to someone of my entomological bent, are the wittiest of all, draw on a long and reverent tradition of sericulture in the Far East.

Sericulture dates back to the early part of the fourth century in Japan and has even more ancient beginnings in China. As should be expected in the light of its long history, traditions and rituals have grown up for every stage of silk production, from the care and feeding of the silkworms to the harvesting of the thread from the cocoons they spin. The worms and also mulberry leaves, which the worms feed upon, are common motifs in Eastern art. In Japan, as late as the 1920s, there was a silkworm god who was honored at family altars when the silkworms finished eating and began to spin.

Resonances of these reverent traditions are lost on an American audience; our agriculture is short on reverence and long on getting directly to the bottom line with hogs, cattle, and soybeans. (There have, however, been moments in American farming history when sericulture became a fad—eighteenth- and nineteenth-century versions of today's boutique agriculture.) Instead, there are other resonances for American buyers. John Pleshette, an actor and writer, who has bought Kadonaga wood and paper pieces, would have liked to buy one of the silk ones, but his wife, he told me, finds anything that has to do with insects repellent, so he didn't. He admitted that the gallery full of them was "kind of eerie," but went on to say, "Still, the impact was so strong because they had been living things. The feeling was there that maybe they weren't dead after all. That was part of the aesthetic. If they weren't insects but cotton balls, say, the pieces would not have had the same impact. I think Kadonaga is taking nature and putting some limits on it but preserving its essential zeitgeist."

The gallery offered Kadonaga's pieces separately—titled collectively

Silk and identified within that collectivity by numbers and letters—at prices ranging from from $300 to $5,000. The most expensive piece that has been sold to date was priced at $2,500. The unsold pieces—many of them large ones, which require a museum setting—are now stored in a studio in downtown Los Angeles which Kadonaga uses as a base for his American visits.

"People feel creepy about bugs anyway," John Pleshette concluded.

......

Richard Boscarino, a New Yorker, knows that, and, as a jewelry maker who once hoped to be an entomologist, and therefore does not find insects creepy at all, he sees his dainty and delicate cockroach art as a joke he is playing on a bug-loathing public. The most outrageous of the jokes is *The Last Supper*. It is a tiny tableau, a three-dimensional recreation of the Leonardo mural, complete with a minutely fringed tablecloth and a cracked wall behind Christ and the disciples, who are represented by cockroaches. "This is my most scandalous still-life," Boscarino says, with a happy grin, "but it's the most popular, and I have made more replicas of it to order than I've made of any other piece."

Boscarino sells his still-lifes—or "roachart," as he also calls them—directly to the public, without benefit of a gallery, for between $300 and $900. He has had one show, à la J. J. Doonesbury, in the men's room at a once popular night spot on Hudson Street called Area, which is now closed.

Boscarino is a slight man of twenty-seven, with dark hair and quick, fine-boned hands. I hope he won't mind my noting that he has a rather buglike quality. I don't think he will, because people say that about me, too, and I don't mind. In the small town where I live, I'm called the Bee Lady—a name I rather fancy. After all, aren't men and women supposed to grow to resemble their mates of many years? To take on characteristics of their pets? And Boscarino has been thinking about bugs for a long time.

Richard Boscarino's speech is precise. He moves rapidly from place to place. He has an easy smile and a happy laugh. He lives in a dark apartment in the West Village, and on a recent Sunday morning when I visited him few of his neighbors were on the streets outside. They were presumably still tucked up with their Arts & Leisure sections of the *Times,* but Boscarino, inside his apartment, enthusiastically spread out a sampling of his work.

One is a replica of a Providence, Rhode Island, diner and is titled *Periplaneta,* the genus name of the cockroaches used in the piece. (They are large American roaches—about an inch and a half long by half an inch across—and he buys them, dead, from the Carolina Biological Supply Company, in Burlington, North Carolina, which offers a large variety of roaches, including the giant hissing cockroach of Madagascar.) The diner, painted a cheerful yellow, has a red floor and contains four booths. Seats at the counter are made of buttons. The cappuccino maker is a .22-caliber shell. The stovepipe is a straw. Lemon meringue pies sit in little brass settings for rhinestones. A cockroach waitress and cook are poised in midbustle serving the roach customers, who sit in the booths and at the counter—including, as Boscarino points out, "a youngster who can barely see over the counter."

Boscarino has collected bugs and been interested in plants since he was a child, when he thought he would become either an entomologist or a botanist. But at twelve he began making jewelry, and after high school he went to the Rhode Island School of Design, in Providence, to get a degree in jewelry making. Today, it is his jewelry that is his main source of income; cockroach art is a sideline.

The pieces grew out of his bug collecting. He had pinned and displayed his specimens, as collectors do, but he found the traditional box displays boring and began to pin out his samples in surroundings as natural as possible. He fixed a cockroach on a piece of kitchen flooring. And then, as his first joke, he made a small table with a crumb on it and sat two roaches on little stools on either side of it. People saw it, were amused, and commissioned him to do other cockroach pieces. His roach boxes make use of his jeweler's skills. *Chez Cafard* (*cafard* means not only hypocrite and a blue mood in French but also cockroach) is an exquisite cockroach-size beauty parlor, with little oval mirrors and pink-and-red striped wallpaper. One cockroach sits under a hair dryer made of a Magic Marker top. Another is having its antennae permed. Still another is being given a French twist by a cockroach hairstylist. A roach replica of a small grocery store has cockroaches shopping for food. Pushing shopping carts made of window screen, they ponder a selection of carrots made from toothpicks, mangoes that are really sesame seeds, broccoli fashioned from cloves. On shelves in the middle of the store, aspirins have been stacked and pencils sliced into rounds to make packaged food. At the checkout counter, a roach pushes buttons made of pinheads on the cash register.

The jeweler-dainty, playfully sardonic, dollhouse quality of Boscarino's work makes its own nervous joke in his current work in progress, *The Pentagon*—a big, unfinished replica of that structure. The Red-Tape Room, with curls of tape surrounding the cockroach staff, looks complete, but in the War Room several cockroach generals waiting to be glued in place lie on their backs, their stiffened legs sticking straight up.

"I always have too many projects," Boscarino says happily. "The dilemma is not enough time to do everything. I wish I could stay awake twenty-four hours a day. I'll take on any commission if it's complicated enough, because I love complexity." Another of his interests is filmmaking, and he took a course in it at N.Y.U. but found it too limiting. In the process, he made a film that became a finalist in the student division of the Academy of Motion Picture Arts and Sciences competition. He used insects in that film, an experiment in macrophotography in which he filled the screen with bugs and kitchen appliances.

To Boscarino's amusement, he has become something of a star. He appeared on *West 57th Street* and *PM Magazine,* and he smiles as he tells about being the featured performer on a popular Japanese television quiz show, *The World in a Nutshell,* three years ago, while celebrities vied with one another to guess the prices of his work. His only regret is that he was filmed in New Haven, not Tokyo.

Although Boscarino likes insects in general, he would not use butterflies, for instance, in his pieces. Butterflies find favor, if any bug does, with the nonentomological public, and he prefers what he calls the "tension" created when he uses an insect that is considered abhorrent. Boscarino's face grows serious as he talks about how adaptable cockroaches are, how good at surviving in a wide range of habitats and conditions, how old a life form they are. "You can't help admiring them," he says.

······

Garnett Puett, the apisculptor, is only one year older than Boscarino. He, too, is a New Yorker and has an entomological background, but with that his similarity to Boscarino ends. Puett is a strong-looking man, muscular from a lifetime of doing heavy beework. He has dark-brown hair, cut short, and brooding brown eyes, which do not follow along when the rest of his face smiles. He has the air of a young man who would not compromise much, and at times he seems to be on the verge of truculence, as is often true of beekeepers. Perhaps this comes from spending so much of one's life away from human concerns.

Puett was born in Hahira, Georgia. His father was a commercial beekeeper and so were his father's father and grandfather. When Puett was a teenager, his father died, and his mother, who was an artist, married Jim Powers. Powers runs what was until very recently the biggest honey-producing operation in the United States. It is based in North Dakota but has branches throughout the continental United States and in Hawaii.

Bees have been a part of Puett's life ever since he can remember, and his stepfather expected him to take over Powers Apiaries when he graduated from college. With that in mind, Puett entered the University of Idaho, to study business administration and entomology. But after a year he switched to art at the University of Washington, in Seattle, specializing in sculpture. At first, he worked with bronze, but he found himself scrapping the finished pieces and thinking about the wax he had used to create them. The process interested him more than the product.

When he graduated, he did not want to go into his stepfather's business, although to this day he does work in the Hawaiian part of the operation when his schedule permits and the bees there need him. He was also, however, disgusted with the art world as he saw it. "Thirty years ago, I understand, it was ninety percent poetry and ten percent sales," he says. "Today, it is just the opposite." He did not want to make the changes in his work which he thought were necessary to create commercially successful sculpture. "I wanted a way to confront viewers with the essence of sculpture—shapes and form," Puett says. "I was willing to frighten them, if necessary, to force them to see." He realized that he could use the forms created by bees for just that purpose. All beekeepers know that the inside of a beehive is beautiful to human eyes, but the patterned structures built by bees from uniform honeycomb cells are seldom seen by any human eyes except beekeepers', and few bee-keepers are expressive enough to convey an idea of that beauty. There-fore, the average gallerygoer should find the forms created by bees fresh and startling enough to make him consider form itself. Or so Puett reasoned. He began by experimenting with beeswax foundation—deli-cate sheets of beeswax, sold by beekeeping-supply companies, that are imprinted in a factory with a matrix of the hexagonal honeycomb pattern that bees build on their own. But he soon switched to using the drawn-out and worked comb itself, with its deeper, cup-shaped cells, completed by the bees.

In 1983, in the face of his stepfather's skepticism and continuing hope that he would decide to manage the Hawaiian division of the business, Puett moved to New York City with a few hundred dollars and a five-year plan. He did not want to live out his life on the fringes of the New York art world, so he gave himself five years within which he must have ten shows and get his work accepted. "If it didn't work out, I would go back to Hawaii and pull honey," he says.

He enrolled in Pratt and got a job delivering art to galleries. In the course of his work, he met gallery owners and artists, and soon he was introduced to two dealers who went on to form the Curt Marcus Gallery, which has handled him ever since. Within two years, he had had his ten shows and was being taken very seriously by the art establishment.

His sculptures, which originally sold for under $1,000, now sell for more than five times that, and there is interest in his work in other parts of the country. Laumeier Sculpture Park, which commissioned his *Apiscaryatid* for $5,000, has been trying to raise another $10,000 to buy it for permanent display.

Critical and commercial acceptance has come so quickly to Puett that those around him are concerned about its effect on his development. Beej Nierengarten-Smith, the director of Laumeier, wonders if he understands how unusual his early success is. After one of Puett's openings, a group of older artists, taking small nibbles from their sour grapes, were speculating about whether it might not have been better for the young man to have a little less luck and a little more struggle. Ann Philbin, who has served as his gallery representative at Curt Marcus, has protected him from exploitation by television. Puett has cooperated with her because he understands that his apisculptures can be played for what he calls their "freak show" aspect, and he *does* want to be considered a serious artist. However, he admits, with an engaging boyish longing, that he would have rather liked to accept an offer to appear on the *Today* show.

Puett and his wife, Whendi, who is a fabric designer, share a large, sunny space in a factory building in Brooklyn, near the Williamsburg Bridge. I visited him there on a clear, sparkling summer day. Along the waterfront, a prostitute waited glumly beside a van with privacy glass, old newspapers fluttered across the streets, and, in among flattened beer cans and old mattresses, some weeds flowered, noticed only by bees and beekeepers. Puett's bees had flown out through a hole in his studio window and were hard at work gathering nectar and pollen.

In his studio, Puett develops the basic forms for his sculptures, usually welding a steel armature, which he will coat with beeswax and give to the bees to finish. Many of the forms are abstract. He sometimes starts with examples from the *Scanning Electron Microscope Atlas of the Honey Bee*, a book of anatomical details so small that they cannot be seen by the unaided human eye. Enlarged, they become pure form. "Nothing relays natural form better than natural form itself," Puett says. He works up these forms on a computer and then welds the armature to express the design in a way that he hopes the bees will accept and use as a base for building comb. If they accept it—and they do in many cases, but not all—they will treat the same form similarly the next time, and Puett will have learned something. (A buyer once displayed a finished sculpture too near a radiator, the wax melted, and the piece was destroyed. Puett gave the armature back to the bees, and they built an identical sculpture upon it.) One of his goals is to create forms so pleasing to bees that they will build on every one.

After coating the armature with beeswax, Puett installs packages of bees, bought from a bee breeder, on the base, which he has enclosed in a box, and there, if the design is acceptable to the bees, they will finish in layered beeswax the sculpture he has begun. When the piece is finished, Puett removes the bees to an ordinary beehive, takes out any honey with a dental water pick, and freezes the sculpture for a short time to kill any wax-moth eggs and larvae that it might contain. Then the piece is enclosed in a glass case—Puett builds one for each of his sculptures—to keep it safe.

Sometimes the forms are human—a head, a row of small figures, or a single figure. In creating the Laumeier *Apiscaryatid,* Puett coated the figure, molded from Whendi's body, with beeswax and set it up last April at the Sculpture Park in a large wooden box with a door on one side for public viewing. He put a caged queen on the figure's head and then released 100,000 bees above the tiny cage. The bees and the viewers were separated by a screen, so that neither would be harmed. Throughout the spring and summer, the bees collected nectar from miles around, drew out the wax on the form into their hexagonal cells, and added to these bases creamy white beeswax of their own making. The cells became the building units for what appear to be layers of shawls draping the head and torso of the waxen form.

The bees' exit and entrance was a small hole in the box behind the figure. The top of the box was also cut away, and was replaced with red Plexiglas. The glowing, warm light that filled the box did not disturb the bees, because their receptivity to the spectrum of visible light is different from ours, and the unusual color skewed and altered the visitors' perception of the figure. According to Nierengarten-Smith, the *Apiscaryatid* quickly became one of the most popular pieces the Sculpture Park has ever exhibited.

I was in St. Louis a number of times during the spring and summer, and I always made a special trip out to the Sculpture Park to see how the bees were coming along. They began by building comb on the top of the figure and worked their way down. By midsummer, although the bees had left the face bare, the rest of the head and the upper torso were covered with layered leaves of wax honeycomb. At summer's end, the queen bee escaped from her cage. Puett was in Hawaii helping to harvest honey at his stepfather's hives, and so was unable to come to Laumeier. As the staff watched, the queen began to lay eggs in the honeycomb cells along the back and one side of the figure. At one point, the bees clustered around the queen in an upper corner of the box, away from the figure, and built more honeycomb there. From the eggs that the queen bee had laid the bees apparently raised themselves some new queens, for during September, just before Puett was to remove the bees from the sculpture, most of the bees in the colony swarmed away with the old queen. When Puett arrived in St. Louis, only a few bees were left on the sculpture, and none of the honey that the colony had gathered remained. He killed the remaining bees and froze the piece in dry ice.

Nierengarten-Smith says she preferred that Puett base his piece on a human form. That is not always to his liking these days, for he wants to move beyond human models, but it is by using a human base for his sculptures that he has attracted the most attention. Reviewing a gallery show of Puett's in *Arts Magazine* for September 1985, Timothy Cohrs writes:

There were so many bees, so many *thousands* of bees, that they stacked up two and three and four deep, dripping from the mass like magma turned into a lifeform. The figure, once it could be identified as such, seemed frozen with shock, stung into a paralysis that at any moment could break and send it and the box and the glass sheet smashing to the ground. The sight of something so primeval, so vital, and so terrifying thrust into the cocoon of the gallery scene was more than surprising—it actually stunned the crowd of art-weary art-watchers at the ArtMart opening into a uniform silence.

Puett's live, untitled piece was planted outside in the gallery's courtyard. It contained over 80,000 honeybees all furiously involved in the process of constructing a hive on the surface of the wax figure. The ceaseless and truly inhuman energy of the piece-in-process contrasted sharply with a finished, bee-less sculpture inside the gallery. . . . the finished piece was absolutely static—no hum, no wild pulse of life, no horrifying vision of a ghastly insect-covered death.

Some viewers have described Puett's work as sadistic—covering a woman's form with bees strikes people to whom bugs are abhorrent as vaguely obscene. Puett shrugs off such reactions. If people think of death and cruelty, he points out, that says more about them than it does about the sculpture. He acknowledges that once he has completed a piece its connotations belong to those who look at it. "But I am not trying to make deathly images," he says, scowling. Puett, after all, comes from a way of life in which having live bees crawl on one's body is not a bad experience (following the Powers Apiaries practice, he works bees without wearing gloves or a protective bee suit) but, rather, a neutral, or even a pleasant, one, standing, as it does, for a benign partnership between bees and human beings. Beekeepers know that bees sting only in exceptional circumstances—circumstances that are easy to control.

Critics have other things to say about Puett's work. Richard Martin writes in *Arts Magazine* for September 1986:

A kouros in wax was transformed by bees into the trunk of a figure as they bored into and dismembered the legs of the figure. Puett takes an especially perverse—and fascinating—interest in this sculpture as an instance of complete change in interaction with the bees. More often, that interaction is more subtle. A striding figure is veiled with the fine net of comb mantilla akin to a sci-fi-movie special effects, yet our transformed monster is a friendly Frankenstein. The initial grotesquery of the figure is quelled and we can see it as the most elegant of transformations.

Writing in *Art in America* for March 1987, Sue Taylor reviews a Chicago show of Puett's and suggests:

The project seemed to comment on the ability of nature to overtake art, to undermine human achievement, inevitably, through time. Indeed, in the face of the bees' urgent, collective activity, human individualism and self-expression suddenly seemed maladaptive quirks in a social system lacking the cooperative base and supreme integration of bee populations.

We are on very slippery anthropomorphic ground here, and to me what is going on seems something much simpler. These Bug Artists are messing around with materials, and that is an interesting thing to be doing. In addition, they're having a rather good time, and that is even better. What their work has to say is something so plain and obvious that it seems surprising that it needs saying at all, but since so many people are engaged in creating artifacts that do say it and no one else is smiling, perhaps it does: we live in a world in which there are many live things other than human beings, and many of these things can seem beautiful and amusing and interesting to us if they can catch our attention and if we can step back from our crabbed and limiting and lonely anthropocentricity to consider them.

(December 1987)

TWELVE

Five-and-Dime Stores

In 1982, Ed Graczyk's play *Come Back to the 5 & Dime, Jimmy Dean, Jimmy Dean* opened in New York City. The setting was a faded dime store in a small Texas town. The title drew not only on fans' yearning for the movie star, who died in 1955, but also on nostalgia for the mercantile establishments that once thrived on Main Streets in towns across the country. The downtown five-and-ten-cent store was already something of a commercial period piece. Today it is relic.

In the autumn of 1993, the Woolworth Corporation announced that it would close 970 of its stores across the country and in Canada, among them nearly half of its 825 remaining variety stores. The closings included what may be the most famous dime store in America, the one in Greensboro, North Carolina, where, in 1960, four black college students sat down at the then segregated counter and ordered lunch, thereby changing history. The Woolworth stores had lost $36 million during the first half of fiscal 1993. "They just hung on too long to many of those

Main Street locations out of affection for the nameplate," said Isaac Lagnado, an industry analyst.

Frank Winfield Woolworth, who opened his first store in 1879 in Utica, New York, prospered as downtown America prospered, but fewer Americans live and shop downtown today. Other merchandising ideas, mart and mall, have captured buyers. But even so, the Woolworth closings were not the "end of the dime-store era," as newspaper feature writers across the country would have it in sentimental pieces about the closing of the local stores. The five-and-dime had ceased to exist soon after Woolworth's death in 1919.

During the founder's lifetime it was a point of honor to keep the top price in his stores at a dime. This despite the fact that his imitators had begun to exceed that limit while continuing to call themselves five-and-ten-cent stores. But after his death, Woolworth's prices began informally inching upward toward the twenty-cent mark. In 1935, the board of directors agreed to discontinue even the twenty-cent limit and let goods be priced as conditions demanded. Their meeting took place in the Woolworth Building in New York under a portrait of the founder, "whose blue eyes and white mustache," writes Woolworth biographer John Winkler, "might have seemed aquiver with resentment."

If any particular year could be singled out as the time of the genuine five-and-dime store, it would probably be 1913. That was when Woolworth, the farm boy who became a millionaire in the best Horatio Alger tradition, proved himself merchant prince by capturing the help of a sitting president, Woodrow Wilson, to press the button that would turn on 80,000 light bulbs in the spanking new Woolworth Tower. Witnessing the event were 800 prominent men who had gathered in the tower's banquet hall to help Woolworth celebrate. Rising to a height of 792 feet and one inch, the building was then the tallest in the world. Woolworth had put $13.5 million into its construction and was bursting with pride over the statement it made.

Frank Woolworth died in 1919, at age sixty-six, owner of 1,050 five-and-tent-cent stores, with an estate valued at $65 million that paid a tax of $1,050,000, the highest on record in New York State at the time. To the man on the street, his fortune, built on nickels and dimes, must have seemed as large as that of Croesus. But that was then and now is now. Today, low-priced variety goods have new merchant royalty. A few months before the Woolworth Corporation closed those 970 stores, *Fortune* magazine announced that the second-richest family in the world was that of Sam Walton, founder of Wal-Mart. With a net worth of $23.5 billion, the Walton clan ranked just behind the sultan of Brunei. In passing, it should be noted that Walton, who died in 1992, has his own monument, albeit something much smaller than the Woolworth Tower. Walton's 5 & 10, in Bentonville, Arkansas, the first store to carry the owner's name, is now preserved, along with its original sign, as a commercial museum dedicated to the later merchant's understanding of the American consumer.

I was born the year the Woolworth directors freed prices in their stores and so I never knew a genuine five-and-dime, yet that was what we called the establishments on Burdick Street in Kalamazoo, Michigan, where I grew up. I can't remember all of the other shops in that bustling downtown, but I can remember S. S. Kresge, F. W. Woolworth, and W. T. Grant. The last-named was too upscale for me. It had been conceived by its founder as a twenty-five-cent store, slipping into a niche between the dime stores and department stores where prices began at fifty cents. But my allowance was only fifteen cents, and I hoarded it over the months to buy Christmas presents at Woolworth's and Kresge's. The stores seemed resplendent to me. I was never allowed to eat in them (my mother insisted that the grease for frying was reused) but I can remember yearning for the doughnuts so temptingly displayed in the Kresge window. They were produced by a machine with a revolving band that dunked them into sizzling fat. They smelled wonderful. When my grades were not what my mother thought they should be I was threatened with the possibility of growing up to become "a dime-store clerk." Secretly I didn't think that was half bad, and pictured myself standing behind one of the open bins of shiny attractive goods at Woolworth's, wearing a rhinestone necklace in the daytime (something else forbidden me).

In 1873, when he was twenty-one years old, Frank Woolworth took a job in a dry-goods store in Watertown, New York, to escape the drudgery of the family farm nearby. He was tall, skinny, his health was frail. He was a bit of an aesthete, inclined toward flute music, and had an air of the theatric. He proved to be a poor salesman but could concoct artful window displays, often using red, the signal color for stores to come, to catch the eye of customers.

Woolworth was first exposed to the idea of a fixed-price store when an acquaintance left Watertown to open a 99-cent store. That man returned on a visit during the 1878 recession and suggested establishing a nickel sales counter at the dry-goods store as a way to perk up business. The store's owner, William H. Moore, reluctantly tried the experiment. He was skeptical because even then nickel goods were cheap—and before the days of mass production they were also shoddy, the kind of stuff that used to be added to a traveling peddler's pack to attract interest in his other wares. And a quality dry-goods store did not want to offer goods that invoked the peddler's image. But the nickel counter did draw customers, and the young Woolworth took notice.

Encouraged by his new wife, Jennie, and fired with the idea of a store in which everything would sell for a nickel, Woolworth opened the Great Five Cent Store in Utica. Business was good at first but then slumped. Woolworth was still confident in the basic soundness of a five-cent store; perhaps the location was wrong. Later the same year he opened a similar store in Lancaster, Pennsylvania, under the original sign. It was augmented with another: WOOLWORTH'S 5-AND-10 CENT

STORE. The young man had added a line of "quality" goods at double the sale price and had thus escaped the notion that he sold only shoddy trinkets. The new store was a success, but Woolworth's biggest problem was finding suppliers of goods he could sell for five-and-ten cents. He realized that if he could place very large orders, he would be able to dictate suppliers' prices, and so he began opening additional stores.

By 1918, just five years after President Wilson pressed the button that lighted the Woolworth Tower, there were 1,000 Woolworth stores, and the chain was expanding to England. Frank Woolworth was a wealthy man. But he was also fat, gorging himself on rich foods, and was growing remote from his business. He was increasingly driven to extravagant personal and public display. His wife, after encouraging and supporting him, had drifted away into some private mental fog. His heirs were waiting in the wings to marry rashly and spend his fortune. He died with his estate in disorder; he had never updated his will and left everything to his wife who was, by that time, a mental incompetent.

If, in a literal sense, the five-and-ten-cent store died with him, it had nevertheless become an important part of American life, and the name lingers on. SPICER'S 5 & 10 says the sign in red and gold on a white store in a sparkling new shopping center in Ladue, Missouri, an affluent suburb west of St. Louis. Ladue is adjacent to another wealthy suburb, Clayton. Max Spicer, who was for a time the manager of a successful Woolworth's, started his own store in Clayton in 1947. Later it was moved to another location in Ladue. After Spicer died in 1970, Jim McNulty, who had worked for him, became owner and president of the store. Over the years he has opened two branches in other suburbs and in 1993 moved his flagship store to the present location.

McNulty, a heavyset man in his forties with an engaging manner, says proudly, "We're number one in the country for dollars spent per square foot in this kind of variety store. We average five hundred dollars annually in sales per square foot. About 150,000 people shop here every year. Our customers are well-to-do and short on time. Yes, we deliver. I started from humble beginnings and worked hard, but I always knew I was going to be rich." A smile spreads across his face. "And now I *am* rich."

His store, brightly lighted, carpeted, contains 6,000 square feet. Its thirty-eight employees, some part-timers, unobtrusively assist customers who want help in selecting just the right party favors or just the right toy. Background music plays. There is an immaculate restroom available for the public, a convenient telephone. I browse past the tin soldiers and the toothbrush shaped like a dinosaur, play with a top, see thumbtacks, tape, typing paper, tote bags, a trapped-rat cat toy. I buy a tiny bottle of beeswax furniture polish and a red plush Father Christmas hat, supported in its own gilt cardboard crown, for my husband to wear on the occasion of his grandson's first Christmas. My purchases, packed into a logoless brown bag, come to $13.73.

Half a continent away, in Maine under another anachronistic sign, THE WINTER HARBOR 5 & 10 is tucked into the small commercial section in the village of the same name. It was opened first in 1972, in a 1923 building that previously housed a grocery and dry-goods store. Pete Drinkwater and his wife, Sandy, bought the store five years ago and live in the apartment above it. A man with a quick and friendly smile, Pete takes me on a tour, shows me the stuffed storage area that once was a butcher's cold room, points out the old meat hooks. I admire the store's creaking oak floors and the cream-colored, pressed-metal ceiling. We visit the basement, brimming on this November day with Christmas goods soon to be displayed. The Drinkwaters' 1,700-square-foot enterprise is jammed with merchandise: bird feeders, Ben-Gay, bells, buoys (this is coastal Maine, after all), brooms, batteries, butcher knives, beaters, baby goods, brushes, and baseball albums.

I ask Drinkwater about the "5 & 10" part of his sign. He laughs. "Well, maybe it's more like five and ten *dollars* today." Drinkwater comes out of a Kresge background. After finishing business college in Bangor, he went to work for the Kmart Corporation into which the Kresge stores had been subsumed. After working in several Kmarts, he was transferred to Upper Darby, Pennsylvania, to manage a Kresge store. "That was one of the two last remaining S. S. Kresge outlets in the country," he says, "and after it closed I was able to take a portrait of S. S. Kresge himself. Let me show it to you." Drinkwater, a young man, dashes upstairs to his apartment and returns lugging a huge, heavily framed likeness of a balding, bushy-browed man in the best founder-of-the-business school of portraiture. "Look at his eyes," Drinkwater says, "they follow you no matter where you stand."

Sebastian Spering Kresge was one of the many men who imitated Woolworth and also gave their names to stores we still lump together and call five-and-dimes: G. C. Murphy, S. H. Kress, J. G. McCrorey, J. J. Newberry. Like Woolworth, many of those men had some Pennsylvania connections. S. S. Kresge was no exception. Born in Bald Mount, Pennsylvania, in 1867, into a frugal Swiss-German family of farmers, the young Kresge also wanted to escape farming life. He struck a bargain with his father: if his father would help him complete his schooling, he would give over to him all the money he would earn until he was twenty-one. With the one exception—an exception almost too touching for a fellow beekeeper to recount—that he could keep all that he could earn selling honey from his hives of bees. During this time, Kresge built up a small apiary of thirty-two hives and "led Monroe County in bee culture," according to his son and biographer, Stanley S. Kresge. His honey sales, together with the money he was able to save from odd jobs and selling tinware, made it possible for him to go into business for himself by the time he was thirty years old.

While working as a traveling salesman, Kresge had met Woolworth and been inspired by him. Rebuffed in his attempt to go into partnership with the man, Kresge instead joined forces with another Pennsylvanian,

J. G. McCrorey, who was later to drop the *e* in his last name and that of his stores. In 1897 they opened a five-and-ten-cent store in Memphis, Tennessee, and shortly after that they opened another in Detroit. Two years later, Kresge exchanged his interest in the Tennessee store for the one in Michigan and began opening other stores to achieve the economies of scale that Woolworth had discovered were necessary. By the time he died in 1966, Kresge owned 930 stores.

In 1913, the year that Woolworth completed his tower, Kresge had more than a hundred stores and issued *Kresge's Katalog of 5¢ and 10¢ Merchandise*. Reprinted in 1975 by Random House, the "katalog" is a delight to browse: a nickel then could buy you a United States flag, an electric egg whip, or two nursing bottles. For a dime you could have a lady's fine ribbed vest, a rosewood pipe, or a child's straw hat.

S. S. Kresge kept his thrifty Swiss-German ways throughout his life, despite the fact that he accumulated enormous personal wealth. The stories about his penuriousness are many. His *New York Times* obituary reports "a pinchpurse attitude . . . was part of the breakup of two of Mr. Kresge's marriages." He wore his shoes until they had holes, then lined them with paper and wore them some more. He once reprimanded his valet for pressing his suit, saying, "Don't you realize they will wear out soon if you do?" But in public matters Kresge was generous. He established a foundation in his name in order "to leave the world a better place than I found it." He followed the initial $1 million endowment with subsequent gifts of more than $60 million. In 1953 Kresge was asked to give a speech at the Harvard University Graduate School of Business, at the dedication of Kresge Hall. He gave what his son Stanley described as the shortest speech on record there. After being introduced, he stood up and said, "I never made a dime talking"—and sat down. I tell Pete Drinkwater this story as we stand admiring the portrait of the man with the following eyes, and he laughs appreciatively.

It has been the competition with mall and mart that has figured importantly in the decline of the old-fashioned dime store. A huge Wal-Mart opened recently in Ellsworth, some thirty miles from Winter Harbor, and I ask Drinkwater how it has affected his business. "Well, thirty miles is a long way to drive for a spool of thread," he replies. "I think what people do is drive over there for their big shopping trips but fill in from my store for incidental items. I don't sell a lot of school supplies before school starts, for instance, but after it has been open for a few days, mothers are in here buying pencils and the notebook paper their kids still need. We can't compete on price, but we can give better service."

The Winter Harbor store provides UPS and fax service, ships fresh lobsters to summer residents in their winter homes, repairs bicycles, takes credit cards, and offers other services, including running downstairs after hours if a customer has a pressing need. "We've increased sales every year I've been here," Drinkwater says, and pauses. "Except this last one. But I think that has to do more with the recession than Wal-Mart."

I put the same question about the effect of the new Wal-Mart to Rick Johnson, a pale, tall young man in his twenties, who for the past year or so has been managing the J. J. Newberry store on Main Street in downtown Ellsworth. Johnson, also a local business-school graduate, worked in four other Newberry's for a year each before coming back home to manage this one, where his mother had clerked for years. In a sense, he has grown up in this store. "We're holding our own," he tells me. "People still like to come in here. They like the look of an old-fashioned store. This is a ten-thousand-square-foot store, not a hundred thousand feet like Wal-Mart, and customers tell me they can find things easier here. Seasonal stuff is the biggest part of our business." He points to the Christmas wreaths and decorations with which clerks are beginning to fill one wall. "There's no place," he adds proudly, "that does as well with Memorial Day flowers as we do."

....

John Josiah Newberry was another of those mercantile Pennsylvani-
ans. Born in 1877 at Sunbury, his first work with dime stores was with
S. H. Kress. In 1911, in Stroudsburg, he opened his first store and soon
began to open others with his brothers, one of whom, C. T. Newberry,
had been superintendent of buyers for Woolworth's. The Newberry
chain remained relatively small; in 1954, the year the founder died, it
consisted of 475 variety stores with sales of $173 million. In 1973 it was
acquired by the Rapid American Corporation, which was in the process
of picking up old-time variety stores.

No one at Rapid American could tell me when this store opened. But
Vincent Donnell of nearby Franklin knew. "My grandfather, Curtis E.
Tracy, built that store," he told me. "Built it in 1934, the year after the
big fire destroyed downtown Ellsworth. It was Ellsworth's first five-and-
ten. Never had anything like it before."

The place is on three levels ascending the sloped street. Upstairs there
are bins of all the usual dime-store goods and, glorious to say, a lunch
counter. I belly up to one of the stools, order a grilled-cheese sandwich,
french fries, and coffee. It's my belief that Mary, the cook and waitress,
does *not* reuse the grease. She is a motherly looking woman and would
probably be horrified at the very idea. I ask her for a receipt, and she tears
off a carton wrapper to write it on. Not many people come here for a
business lunch, I guess, although all the stools are full.

Having satisfied one forbidden childhood yearning, I decide to fulfill
another and sashay over to the jewelry counter. Rhinestones are out of
fashion, it seems, but I find a pretty pair of dangly silver earrings. They
cost five dollars, but I buy them anyway. I walk out into the crisp
November sunshine. My mood is buoyant and I notice I am humming
the 1920s Billy Rose song, "I Found a Million Dollar Baby in a Five and
Ten Cent Store."

(June 1994)

THIRTEEN

Earthquake Fever

On Monday, 3 December 1990, there was no earthquake along the New Madrid Seismic Zone, an ancient weakness in the earth's crust which runs crookedly for 125 miles from northern Arkansas to southern Illinois, alongside the Mississippi River. Iben Browning, an inventor, business consultant, and self-taught climatologist, had said there was a one-in-two chance that on or about that date a major earthquake would occur in the area. No, said government and academic earthquake specialists: the chance was more like one in 60,000.

It was a nonearthquake about which no one was wrong. Browning could take comfort in the *other* one out of two, and the academics and government people could take pride in their 59,999. Of course, it's not quite true that no one was wrong. The St. Louis psychic who said that the earthquake would happen at the end of November, perhaps on Thanksgiving weekend, was wrong. A man named Jacques called in to a Rolla, Missouri, radio show and said that the earthquake would take place on Tuesday, 4 December, because earthquakes were triggered by underground nuclear explosions, and his research showed that those explosions always happened on Tuesdays. He was wrong. So was Larry Evans, who wrote a letter to the editor of the New Madrid *Weekly Record* in which he said that while praying he had received the information that the earthquake would be at ten in the morning on 2 December. And so were the coffee drinkers in cafés who scribbled with ballpoint pen "1234567890" on paper napkins, circling the first two numerals for December, the next for the day. Four fifty-six was the time of the magnitude 7.8 earthquake. And then they would proudly circle the last digits, the nine and the zero, for the year.

I have a farm about a hundred miles from New Madrid, Missouri, which is in the middle of the New Madrid Seismic Zone. The zone is a seismically active area, and geologists expect that it will someday produce an earthquake of the dimensions of a series of earthquakes that took place there in the winter of 1811–12, which were among the most severe to have occurred on the North American continent in historical times and also among the most severe ever to have taken place on the planet. The zone continually acts up. There are several hundred earthquakes along it every year, most of them too small to be felt. But one afternoon some years ago I was standing in my living room and felt the floor jiggle beneath my feet. It made me distinctly queasy to have my most basic assumptions about the solidity and rightness of the world denied by the earth's turning to Jell-O. I learned later from the radio news that the earthquake was in the New Madrid Seismic Zone.

I first heard of Browning's prediction early in December of 1989. Browning had spoken at the Missouri Governor's Conference on Agriculture, held at Osage Beach from the tenth to the twelfth of December. News reports identified Browning as a climatologist from Albuquerque who claimed to have predicted the destructive San Francisco Bay area earthquake of the previous October. His new prediction was unsettling.

I hadn't known that it was possible to predict earthquakes. I wondered if he could really do it. And, if so, how?

I telephoned Browning in early March of last year. He sounded wary and defensive, and made it clear that he didn't like to talk to journalists, but he did explain to me that his "projection" (he bristled at the word "prediction") was based on tidal forces. On 3 December 1990, he told me, the sun and the moon would be in line with the earth, creating high tidal forces. "And high tidal forces trigger the eruption of volcanoes—I'm a vulcanologist, really; this earthquake business is just a sideline—and earthquakes," he said. I told him I found that interesting and would like to see some documentation of the projection of the San Francisco earthquake before it happened. "If you want to know what the scientific community thinks of my work, you can ask David Stewart, the director of the Center for Earthquake Studies, in Cape Girardeau, Missouri," he responded, side-stepping my request. "He'll tell you how much my work is worth. And those other details . . . Well, I'm retired now, and my daughter, Evelyn, is editing my newsletter. You can talk to her." He handed the telephone over to Evelyn Browning Garriss. I needed some proof of her father's "projections," I told her. "Oh, you want something on his methods?" she asked. Well, yes, that, too. But it would be really important to show that he had mentioned the earthquakes *before* they happened, I explained. She took down my name and address and promised to send me a packet of information. It never came.

Soon a tape of Browning's speech which I had requested from the Missouri Agriculture Department arrived, and I was able to hear him say, "December third, 1990, at thirty degrees north latitude, there will be the highest tidal force in twenty-seven years. . . . We are back in the same triggering-force configuration as of December third next year as we were when the great New Madrid earthquake went off. Will it go off? . . . If you pull a trigger on a gun it goes off only if it is loaded. . . . Certainly the opportunity exists for it to be loaded, because a hundred thousand cubic miles of dirt or so has washed off of this part of the world down to and is now constituting the Mississippi River delta. So there has been an enormous load taken off this part of the plate." He also entertained the audience with jokes about journalists and communism. And he spoke about the theory of the greenhouse effect: "Fundamentally, it's garbage." Browning believed instead that the planet is cooling. "By 2010 . . . the Mississippi will normally freeze over down to about Natchez." He tied historic cold periods to political unrest and predicted that the near future would be a time of famine, revolution, and war.

In May, I drove over to New Madrid to look around. New Madrid was laid out in 1789 by George Morgan, a Revolutionary War patriot who had grown disillusioned about the new republic's chances of survival. Working with Spanish settlers in New Orleans, Morgan drew up plans for a large city, a strategic metropolis, on the Mississippi River, which would be controlled by the king of Spain. The spot he chose was L'Anse à la Graisse (Cove of Grease, so called because of the fat bear and buffalo that could be hunted nearby), and, hoping to ingratiate himself with the king, he named the town New Madrid. There were difficulties. Morgan lost interest and returned to the East. The town survived, but not on the scale that Morgan had dreamed of. The Spanish built a fort, levied duties on river traffic, and by century's end the sandy bluffs along the river were home to six hundred people inured to fighting ague and floods.

That original New Madrid crumbled into the river during the 1811–12 earthquakes. The New Madrid of today is slightly to the north of the original site, in the part of Missouri called the bootheel, hunkered down behind the earthen levee that protects it from the Mississippi. Yellow flowers—hop clover, cinquefoil, and dandelions—were blooming on the levee the day I was there. They looked cheerful, but the river—muddy, powerful, turbulent, ominous—did not. Next to the levee is a historical museum, housed in a nineteenth-century brick building that was originally the First and Last Chance Saloon, a stopping point for thirsty riverboat men. In it are displays relating to Indians, to New Madrid's role in the Civil War, and to the great earthquakes. The museum does a brisk business in earthquake T-shirts (IT'S OUR FAULT and VISIT HISTORIC NEW MADRID WHILE IT'S STILL THERE). A docent told me that she was aware of Browning's prediction but didn't credit it. "We're used to earthquakes," she said. "We have five a week. Had one yesterday. I've lived here all my life, and I never even heard about those big ones until I was all the way grown up." The center of town looks rundown and shabby, and many of the stores along Main Street are empty. But beyond them are the well-tended houses of the town's 3,300 residents, many of whom work for the Noranda Aluminum smelting plant or for Associated Electric cooperative, a power-generating station, or for the A. C. Riley Cotton Company. This is primarily an agricultural town. Soybeans, corn, and cotton grow in the flat, alluvial bottomland that surrounds it.

That day, high winds blowing over the plowed fields turned the air yellow with dust. I drove on down to the Mississippi River Crossing—past Portageville, which was originally Shin Bone and is now the home of the annual National Soybean Festival. I wanted to see Reelfoot, the lake created by the earthquake, on the Tennessee side of the river, catty-corner from New Madrid. Part of Reelfoot is now a Federal Wildlife Refuge, and the day I was there it was specializing in great blue herons. The lake is fourteen miles long, five miles wide, and eighteen feet deep, with something about it that reminded me of an Army Corps of Engineers project. I had read an account of a hunter and trapper who was present at the time of the earthquake. He told of great fissures appearing and the ground sinking. I tried to imagine the sound and shudder made by the land as it gave way.

One Indian legend has it that Kalopin, or Reelfoot, was a Chickasaw chief with a clubfoot, who fell in love with a Choctaw princess named Laughing Eyes. Her father refused to let him have her, so he abducted her, despite a dream he'd had in which he was warned that the earth would rock in anger and the waters would swallow his village. During the marriage ceremony, the earth began to roll in rhythm with the tomtoms, and the Father of Waters roared over the village. Under Reelfoot Lake, the legend says, lie the bodies of Reelfoot, his people, and Laughing Eyes.

But the Creek said otherwise. They said that when Tecumseh, the great Shawnee chief, was trying to form a federation of tribes to stop the white men from taking their lands he grew weary of their indecision and warned, in the autumn of 1811, that he would leave them and in thirty days' time would stamp his foot. He did so, and the earth rumbled and split, and then they knew that the Great Spirit had sent him.

The logarithmic Richter scale for measuring the magnitude of earthquakes was not developed until 1935, and so could not be used to measure the 1811–12 earthquakes. But the modified Mercalli scale, which measures the severity of an earthquake in a particular area—how many houses were destroyed, how much sand and mud were ejected from the earth—can be applied, using contemporary descriptions. It is expressed in Roman numerals, I through XII. The XII stands for total destruction and corresponds roughly to the high eights on the Richter scale. The great 1906 San Francisco earthquake, for example, was a VII. Starting on 16 December 1811, and extending through the following February, the New Madrid Seismic Zone experienced at least three earthquakes that are rated XI and one that is rated XII. In between, and for months afterward, there were almost constant smaller shocks. Samuel Mitchill, who was a professor of natural history and a senator from New York, collected eyewitness reports of the earthquakes, and told of a Dr. Robertson, living in nearby St. Genevieve, who recorded more than 500 tremors and "then ceased to note them any more, because he became weary of the task."

In the western third of North America, the convoluted folds of the earth's surface and its fractured geologic structure tend to absorb the seismic energy of an earthquake. Even an 8.5 earthquake in Los Angeles, say, would fade by the time it reached San Francisco, some 400 miles away. But in the eastern two-thirds of the continent the same energy travels more easily. Below the New Madrid Seismic Zone lies a deeply buried rift in the continental plate, a weakened spot where the earth's crust once started to pull apart. The rift is under stress from tectonic forces. A trough above the rift has, over millions of years, filled with gravel and sand. During those 1811–12 earthquakes, water mingled with the soft substrate and turned it into something resembling quicksand—a process called liquefaction. Seismic waves moved up through the mixture and through the solid slab that is the surface of the eastern two-thirds of the continent. The earthquake, first felt in New Madrid on 16 December, disturbed Washington, D.C., more than 800 miles away. According to Mitchill, "a gentleman standing in his chamber at his desk and writing, in the third story of a brick house, upon the Capitol Hill, suddenly perceived his body to be in motion, vibrating backward and forward, and producing dizziness." Tremors were also reported as far away as Boston and northern Canada. Judge James Witherell, of Michigan, told Mitchill that Indians living on an island in a lake outside Detroit saw the waters of the lake appear to "tremble and boil like a great pot over a hot fire; and immediately a vast number of large tortoises rose to the surface, and swam rapidly to the shore, where they were taken for food." All told, tremors were felt over an area of a million square miles—half of the United States.

There is no lack of firsthand reports from New Madrid itself, for nearly everyone there survived. Understandably, the accounts vary according to the place where the witness was shortly after 2:00 A.M. on 16 December, when the first shock hit, but all the witnesses speak of feeling terror and nausea as the earth heaved, and describe the earth being torn apart, the elements mingling in a frightening way, and hearing sharp noises and rumbling ones as the earth spewed sulfurous gases, sand, and coal. The air, thick and malodorous, was colored by flames from small cabins collapsing into hearth fires. The Mississippi River roiled and roared, swallowing the sandy bluffs as they fell into it, running against the normal current as it rushed to spread back into new holes and crevices, creating waterfalls where they had never been. A comprehensive summary of eyewitness accounts, collected by Timothy Flint, was published in Boston in 1826. Flint wrote:

The shock of these earthquakes must have equalled in their terrible heavings of the earth, any thing of the kind that has been recorded . . . Whole tracts were plunged into the bed of the river. The grave-yard at New Madrid, with all its sleeping tenants, was precipitated into the bend of the stream. Most of the houses were thrown down. Large lakes were made in an hour. Other lakes were drained . . . and when the water disappeared a stratus of land . . . was left in its place. The trees split in the midst, lashed one with another, and are still visible over large tracts of country, inclining in every direction and at every angle to the earth and the horizon. They described the undulation of the earth as resembling waves, increasing in elevation as they advanced, and when they attained a certain fearful height, the earth would burst, and vast volumes of water and sand and pit-coal were discharged, as high as the tops of the trees. I have seen a hundred of these chasms which remained fearfully deep although in a very tender alluvial soil, and after a lapse of seven years, whole districts were covered with white sand so as to become uninhabitable. The water at first covered the whole country. The birds themselves lost all power and disposition to fly, and retreated to the bosoms of men. A few persons sunk in to chasms and were providentially extricated. One person died of affright . . . A bursting of the earth just below the village of New Madrid arrested this mighty stream in its course and caused a reflux of its waves, by which in a little time a greater number of boats were swept by the ascending current . . . and left upon the dry earth. . . . They remark that the shocks were clearly distinguishable into two classes; those in which the motion was horizontal, and those in which it was perpendicular. The latter were attended with explosions, and the terrible mixture of noises, that preceded and accompanied the earthquakes, in a louder degree, but were by no means so desolating and destructive as the other.

Modern earthquake deaths and injuries are caused by the collapse of modern structures. The chimneys of the hundred or so low cabins in New Madrid collapsed as they, and the church and schoolhouse, crumbled, but few people died, even in the boats on the river. Including the person who died of "affright," fewer than a dozen deaths were reported in all accounts.

In the summer, I went to Washington, D.C., and, using the research facilities at the Library of Congress, read through the geological literature on the New Madrid Seismic Zone and tidal-force theory. By also reading the New Madrid *Weekly Record,* the *St. Louis Post-Dispatch,* and my own Ozark hometown newspaper, I was able to follow, with increasing amazement, the growth of earthquake fever.

Every day, the moon exerts a steady, smooth gravitational pull on the earth as it moves in its orbit. On the oceans, where there is no obstruction, it tugs the waters and causes tides. On land, the response is not so dramatic, but there is still a small, measurable bulge, nowhere more than one foot high, pulled along by the moon. When the sun is aligned with the moon, which, on 3 December 1990, was at its nearest approach to the earth since 1912, the total gravitational force is only a little stronger than it is the rest of the time. The strain that was put on the New Madrid Seismic Zone on 3 December can be measured and is represented by the number 1.186×10^8. That number is interesting only when it is compared with the strain peak on the New Madrid Seismic Zone on 17 January 1988, another date of high tidal force: the figure then was 1.177×10^8, only slightly smaller. There was no big earthquake on 17 January 1988, either. To put it another way, the strain over and above that during a normal high tide is analogous to the change in air pressure you would feel during a slow ride down in an elevator from the top floor of a ten-story building.

Nevertheless, we have all sat on beaches contemplating the tides, and it seems intuitively obvious that a force that can shift that much water *should* be able to release the chthonic power of an earthquake. Browning's theory of tidal-force triggers is not new. My 1890 *Encyclopedia Britannica* discusses it, and assigns its "recent" formulation to Alexis Perrey, of Dijon. It is not rare, either: the *Old Farmer's Almanac* states flatly that the five days around high tides are the most likely ones for earthquakes in the Northern Hemisphere. The theory has occurred to scientists, too, and they have studied the correlation of tidal maxima with earthquakes. I called an old friend who is a geologist—Tom Simkin, a volcano expert at the Smithsonian Institution—after I discovered that he had contributed material to an ad-hoc group of eleven geologists who reviewed Browning's "projection" for the National Earthquake Prediction Evaluation Council, an advisory committee to the United States Geological Survey. He sent me a 1973 paper he had co-written pointing up a startling correlation between tidal peaks and earthquakes coming after the collapse of a volcanic caldera in the Galápagos Islands. I began to accumulate other papers that showed positive correlations.

I phoned Brian Mitchell, the chairman of the Department of Earth and Atmospheric Sciences at St. Louis University—also a member of the ad-hoc group—whose specialty is the New Madrid Seismic Zone. I asked him about the studies. "The trouble is that they show a variety of correlations," he said. "Some are with tidal maxima, and some with times in between. A number of them are based on erroneous data or contain mistakes in the calculation of data." He recommended that I talk to Thomas Heaton, still another member of the ad-hoc group, who is the seismologist in charge of the U.S.G.S. office in Pasadena and is a specialist in tidal theory.

"Well, it's hard," Heaton told me when I asked him about the correlations. "There are some late papers that show a correlation with earthquakes and tidal forces and some late papers that don't show a correlation. For instance, in 1975 I wrote a paper that showed that, while for earthquakes worldwide there was no correlation, for shallow earthquakes with a vertical component there was a slight correlation. But then I redid the data and found that under stricter statistical conditions there wasn't *any* correlation. So in 1982 I published another paper, saying, in effect, 'Never mind.' Browning cites my first paper in support of his theory but never mentions my second."

The ad-hoc evaluators had asked Browning about the omission. One of them, Ira Satterfield, from the Missouri Department of Natural Resources, in Rolla, talked about it on the local public-radio station on 30 November. He said, "We asked Browning in our telephone conversations, 'Why don't you refer to Dr. Thomas Heaton's latest publication on this instead of his earliest one?' His reply was, 'It doesn't fit my situation.' "

During my talk with Heaton, I asked him if the 1811–12 earthquakes at New Madrid had happened at a time of high tidal forces. He rummaged through some papers, and said, "On 16 December 1811, there was a peak tidal force, but not as high as one in 1809. There was an even higher one in December 1813. 23 January and 7 February 1812, the dates of the big subsequent earthquakes, were not on tidal peaks at all." About all that can be said is that some earthquakes happen on tidal peaks. But tidal peaks happen without earthquakes. They can't be used as predictors.

By autumn, Iben Browning was refusing all requests for interviews, and the man he had referred me to, David Stewart, proved nearly as elusive. "Out" or "Busy" was the answer I got when I telephoned his office, and he did not return my calls. Stewart *was* busy. He was the source that journalists from all over the country and from some other countries as well were going to when, in that newspaperly tradition of evenhandedness, they wanted a quote to counter the uniformly negative comments they were receiving from other geologists on the Browning prediction. In addition to giving quotes to the *Times,* the *Chicago Tribune, The Wall Street Journal,* and *The Manchester Guardian,* Stewart was putting out news releases of his own about earthquake preparedness, talking to groups, and training others to talk to groups. I saw a picture of him in the New Madrid *Weekly Record* briefing Marilyn Quayle, the wife of the vice president, on the New Madrid Seismic Zone. But in early October his associate director, Michael Coe, who was formerly the head of the earthquake program at the Missouri Emergency Management Agency and had been reassigned to Stewart's office to help with the press of business, did phone me. He was able to answer a few questions, but referred me to Stewart for most of them. Stewart, however, was out of the office; he was visiting Browning. Browning himself had apparently had his fill of interviews; a British production company called TAN-STAAFL (There Ain't No Such Thing as a Free Lunch) put out a 100-minute video that was billed as his final and farewell interview. It had been advertised for ninety-nine dollars in several Midwestern newspapers under the words A MAJOR EARTHQUAKE HAS BEEN PROJECTED BY DR. IBEN BROWNING TO STRIKE THIS AREA DECEMBER 3, 1990, and the ad featured an endorsement by Stewart: "He is, perhaps, the most intelligent man I've ever met."

In the TANSTAAFL videotape I was able to see that Browning is a corpulent man with glasses, a pale complexion, and short-cropped hair who speaks with assurance as he hands out snippets of highly complex information from such an array of fields that it is difficult for a viewer to evaluate his conclusions. Browning was born in Texas in 1918 and was a precocious child. He graduated from Southwest Texas State Teachers College at nineteen with a degree in mathematics. He was a test pilot during World War II and spent his off hours reading the *Encyclopedia Britannica.* "I read articles at random, integrating them into what I already knew," he told an interviewer. After the war, he accumulated graduate degrees in the biological sciences from the University of Texas, worked as a researcher in a variety of defense-contract companies, and became an inventor, an author, and a business consultant. He is married. His daughter, Evelyn Garriss, who assists him, has an academic background in history. Now, at seventy-three, he suffers from complications of diabetes. He told one interviewer that he would be surprised to still be alive on 3 December. (He was.) He received countrywide fame as a speaker at Blanchard's New Orleans Investment Conferences, beginning in 1985. These are annual conferences, organized by James Blanchard, the founder of the National Committee to Legalize Gold, and a conservative who would like to see the United States return to the gold standard. His self-confessed heroes are Ayn Rand and Barry Goldwater, both of whom have spoken at the conferences. Other speakers have been Milton Friedman and, in 1990, along with Garris, Arnaud de Borchgrave, the editor of the conservative *Washington Times*. The conferences are attended by private investors who don't like to put their money into the hands of brokers. Much of the TANSTAAFL video is taken up with advice from Browning and his daughter about investments in agriculture futures and the like, which are supposed to be made attractive by Browning's insistence that the earth is entering a period of colder weather. The press has routinely reported that Browning is a consultant to Paine-Webber, but he has not been one for the past two years. He was one of "fifteen or so" consultants, and the only climatologist, who were used by PaineWebber for about ten years, according to Judith Seime, a research assistant at PaineWebber's Chicago office. She would not venture an estimate of the accuracy of his predictions.

Browning predicts lots of things. In the TANSTAAFL video he says that by 2050 half the world's population will have died from AIDS, and that in a thousand years it will have become an unimportant disease, like measles. In a book published in 1981, *Past and Future History*, Browning has a nine-page list of "inferred" events that will take place between 1980 and 2010. Among them are the following:

Canada will cease to export grain because the climate will get too cold.
Egypt has a 50% chance of having its Aswan Dam removed by atomic bombs.
Arizona will be wetter than in the last 1000 years. [Right so far.]
Feudalism will sweep the earth.
Eastern Europe will break out of Russian control.
France will be deeply involved in retaking an Empire.
Nineteen eighty-six at 30 degrees south latitude and 1990 at 30 degrees north latitude will be exceptional years for earthquakes and volcanoes. [Wrong.]
Quantitative people will have high enough skills to go to robotic slaves but the humanistic people will turn to human slaves.

The TANSTAAFL video includes an intercut earlier interview purporting to show that Browning did indeed predict the San Francisco earthquake. That tape, according to the interviewer, was made in Albuquerque on 16 September 1989, one month and one day before the earthquake. During that portion of the video, a message in block letters fills the screen: "Dr. Browning warns of earthquake activity on or about 16 October, 1989. San Francisco earthquake occurred 17 October, 1989." But what Browning is actually saying behind those suggestive words is the following: "As of October 16, 1989, there will be a full moon. It's a 413-day precursor high tidal force of the high tide of December 3, 1990. And there'll be earthquakes go off and perhaps a volcano or two. . . ." There are earthquakes someplace in the world nearly every day. Browning's prediction, which left size and location unspecified, would have seemed impressive only to someone who didn't know of their frequency. Most news reports said that Browning "claimed" to have predicted the San Francisco earthquake, but the word "claim," like the journalistic "alleged," is passed over by many readers. One reporter, William Robbins, of the *Times,* tried to substantiate the claim. He called a man who said he had heard Browning in a speech forecast the San Francisco earthquake, but the devastating magnitude 7.1 earthquake and the grim TV pictures that followed may have given Browning's words more specificity in the man's memory than they actually had. The ad-hoc group obtained a transcript of the speech and found that he had said only that there would probably be "several earthquakes around the world, Richter 6 plus, and there may be a volcano or two"—little more than he said in the taped interview on the video. Over the past ten years, there has been an annual average of a hundred and ten earthquakes of magnitude 6 or greater, working out to about one in any given three-day period. Browning's was a safe forecast, worldwide.

Who, I wondered, had given Browning his pulpit at the Missouri Governor's Conference on Agriculture, where all this started? That person, I found out, was Tom Hopkins, an employee of the Missouri Department of Agriculture and the coordinator of the conference. I talked to him in late October 1990. "Well, this is the way it worked," he told me. "Before I get programs ready for these conferences, I ask around. Bill Galbraith—he's with the North American Equipment Dealers Association—he told me about this guy Browning. He said he'd spoken at one of their meetings about ten years ago and had made a bunch of predictions. Some of the guys kept track and a lot of them came true. Some say he's a quack, though. So I went to my boss, Charlie Kruse"—Missouri's Director of Agriculture—"and his reaction was 'You got to be kidding. We're not going to have some climatologist witch doctor at the conference.' But I convinced him. I said 'Trust me, Charlie.' I was talking to Dr. Browning just last Friday. I called him to see if we could schedule his daughter to come to speak at this year's conference, on December 9th to the 11th. He said, 'Well, if what I think is going to happen does happen, you aren't going to have a conference, but we'll book her.' And I said to him, 'There better be an earthquake on December 3rd or when she comes in the room everyone is going to say "Quack, quack." ' And he said, 'Tom, what we're saying is going to happen will happen, maybe on December 3rd, maybe January 1st, but it's going to happen.' "

Academic and government geologists and geophysicists were put in a difficult position by the Browning prediction. They knew that the New Madrid Seismic Zone was active and potentially dangerous; they had been trying for years to alert the public and improve building standards. But they didn't believe that anyone could forecast the day of an earthquake. On the other hand, they couldn't guarantee that there *wouldn't* be an earthquake on 3 December. Geology is not a laboratory science; events cannot be repeated, or conditions altered. Geology's time span allows for no such neat experiments. Geologists speak of probabilities for earthquakes over large periods of time. Arch Johnston, the director of the Center for Earthquake Research and Information at Memphis State University, is a New Madrid Seismic Zone specialist and was also a member of the ad-hoc group. He has spent as much time as anyone has thinking about the potential for another devastating New Madrid earthquake, and has worked out the probabilities, on the basis of seismic data and the slim geohistorical record. The geologic evidence shows that there have been some very large earthquakes in the New Madrid Seismic Zone in times past. But, although there are hundreds of small earthquakes there every year, since the series of earthquakes during the winter of 1811–12 there has been only one large one—a IX, in 1895. In working out the probability of the occurrence of such an earthquake, Johnston and his colleague Susan Nava, in a 1985 paper, remind the reader, "The probability estimates . . . rely on the assumption that the New Madrid Seismic Zone generates major earthquakes in a repeated fashion."

I asked Brian Mitchell, at St. Louis University, about this assumption. "It is basic to the analysis of earthquakes," he said. "It is as good an assumption as can be made. Geologic evidence from trenching through a part of the fault shows earthquakes that have caused liquefaction in the substrate, which indicates that there have been at least two previous severe earthquakes. These cannot be precisely dated but one may have occurred from six hundred to one thousand years ago and the other from six hundred to a thousand years before that." In the spring of 1990, in plenty of time for anyone who wanted a comparison with the Browning prediction, the U.S.G.S. published a circular, "Tecumseh's Prophecy: Preparing for the Next New Madrid Earthquake," which, using John-ston's work and that of others, estimated with appropriate scholarly caution that the probability that an earthquake of magnitude 6 to 6.5 would occur in the New Madrid Seismic Zone in the next fifteen years was somewhere between 16 and 63 percent.

This isn't fun. This doesn't send a little thrill of fear down the spine. This doesn't get people excited over earthquake preparedness. This doesn't get you on the evening news. What does do those things is the firmed-up Browning prediction that came out of a memo written by David Stewart last summer after an earlier visit to Browning. The memo was addressed to a number of geologists, but it circulated widely in Missouri state offices and in the press. In it Stewart accepts Browning's successful prediction record and praises Browning's abilities. It is here that Stewart makes the comment about Browning's intelligence which was used in the advertisement for the TANSTAAFL video. Stewart admits that he does not understand how Browning picks the particular spot where an earthquake will occur on a day of high tidal force. (According to Satterfield, that turned out to be simple. When asked about it by the ad-hoc group, Browning replied, "Well, like you-all, I read the paper," and went on to explain that he watched to see where geologists were spending money doing research.) In the memo Stewart gave the predic-tion greater specificity. He said that Browning was concerned about earthquakes on 3 December 1990, plus or minus two days, on the Hay-ward Fault (in California), in the New Madrid Seismic Zone, and in

Tokyo. The memo went on to say, "He would assign a 50% chance to each of these, independent of the other, and in the aggregate an 87% probability that at least one of these three will go December 3. He is virtually 100% certain that some major quake will occur in that band of latitudes on or about that date." Those percentages, unlike the less exciting ones from the U.S.G.S., turned up frequently in news reports thereafter.

Mark Twain never wrote about the New Madrid earthquake, but he did write about the Mississippi River and the kinds of conclusions that the study of it can lead to. In *Life on the Mississippi* Twain described how the river, in its convoluted, curling path, sometimes cut a new channel through an oxbow. Such a cutoff was important to river pilots, for it could save them miles. He documents several cutoffs that he knew of from his own piloting days and a number that had been recorded over the years. And then he writes:

In the space of one hundred and seventy-six years the Lower Mississippi has shortened itself two hundred and forty-two miles. That is an average of a trifle over one mile and a third per year. Therefore, any calm person, who is not blind or idiotic, can see that in the Old Oolitic Silurian Period, just a million years ago next November, the Lower Mississippi was upward of one million three hundred thousand miles long, and stuck out over the Gulf of Mexico like a fishing-rod. And by the same token any person can see that seven hundred and forty-two years from now the Lower Mississippi will be only a mile and three-quarters long and Cairo and New Orleans will have joined their streets together, and be plodding comfortably along under a single mayor and a mutual board of aldermen. There is something fascinating about science. One gets such wholesome returns of conjecture out of such a trifling investment of fact.

My copy of the Stewart memo is from a state office, and someone has underlined a section of it that mentions bridges collapsing on the Mississippi and the military coming in with pontoon bridges. Someone has scrawled "Very interesting" across the top of the memo. Bureaucracies, public and private, fired up their Wats lines and Xerox machines and began holding meetings, conducting earthquake-preparedness seminars and drills, and issuing information to help the public prepare quickly for a destructive earthquake. Schools announced plans to close on 3 December. In the autumn, minor tremors along the seismic zone, the sort that would not have rated even a mention in years past, provided the news pegs to hang stories on in newspapers and news magazines across the country. The New Madrid Seismic Zone made *Time, Newsweek,* and national television. The United States Figure Skating Association, which was scheduled to begin its regional competition on 3 December in St. Louis, postponed the meet. My hometown newspaper reported that a pair of state troopers, authoritative, shiny, and trim in their uniforms, had given a talk about this man who had correctly predicted the San Francisco earthquake and who now said that there was a 50-to-80-to-100 percent chance of a big earthquake, maybe in New Madrid. They urged survival preparedness for the entire town.

In mid-October, the ad-hoc group's evaluation of Browning's prediction was released at a news conference and widely reported. Using the data Browning had provided for them, the committee members had tested his methods and found them no better than random guessing for predicting earthquakes, or, as one panel member, Duncan Agnew, said, "You could select the dates by throwing darts at a calendar, and you would do as well as Dr. Browning did." They also examined his track record. "This was important," Arch Johnston told me in discussing the report. "Even if his science wasn't valid, if he had accurately predicted seismic events—well, then, perhaps he knew something we didn't." They examined his claim to have predicted not only the San Francisco earthquake but other earthquakes and also volcano eruptions, and found in every case no evidence to support the claim.

In the TANSTAAFL video the interviewer asked Browning why it was that his work was not accepted by government or academic scientists. "I don't have any interaction with the government or academia," Browning replied. "I deal with people who solve problems, not people who make problems." And when the ad-hoc group asked him for his policy recommendations his written reply was "As to policy—I strongly recommend against one. The government has an unblemished record of screwing up everything it touches."

Stories about the ad-hoc group's news conference were followed, on 21 October, by a story discrediting Browning's chief supporter, David Stewart. According to the *Post-Dispatch*, Stewart had been involved in an analogous earthquake scare in North Carolina in the 1970s, this one involving a psychic. After the furor over that failed prediction died down, Stewart had been denied tenure at the University of North Carolina, where he taught geology. A few days after the *Post-Dispatch* story appeared, Stewart issued a statement saying he would no longer talk about Browning. He left a message for me with his secretary which said, "There is nothing true about the *St. Louis Post-Dispatch* story of 21 October." But Stewart had cut a swath in the press in North Carolina, and a trail of news stories and interviews seemed to corroborate the *Post-Dispatch* story.

According to these, Stewart, who is a fifty-three-year-old Missourian, grew up hoping to be a minister, but while he was attending Missouri's Central Methodist College he found that his belief in reincarnation clashed with Methodism, and he dropped out of school. He hitchhiked around the country and ended up in an ashram near San Diego. One day, while he was practicing yoga, a message came to him to leave, to marry the woman with whom he believed himself to have been linked in another life, and to have five children. He did these things in the process of building a career and acquiring a Ph.D. in geophysics from the University of Missouri at Rolla. In 1971, he went to teach at the University of North Carolina at Chapel Hill, and became a popular professor. In 1975, he picked up a copy of the *National Enquirer* that told about supposedly successful earthquake predictions made by a psychic named Clarissa Bernhardt. (She also predicted that Nelson Rockefeller would become President in 1976, that Queen Elizabeth would abdicate, and that Johnny Carson would be a blackmail victim.) Impressed, Stewart invited Bernhardt to North Carolina to give a reading of the state's seismological condition. Using an airplane, Stewart and Bernhardt toured the state. Afterward, Bernhardt predicted that the Wilmington area would have a magnitude 8 earthquake within a year of her visit and most likely within a few days of 17 January 1976, a date that Stewart later said he had pressed her for. This prediction badly frightened the area's residents, because the Wilmington area was the site of a nuclear power plant. The earthquake did not happen. In 1977, after Stewart was denied tenure, he told an interviewer, "I have now discovered that science does not even touch the truth. . . . I may or may not remain active in the geologic sciences. Probably not. It was an interim thing in my life. I'll probably spend full time in the childbirth movement." After a tenure-decision appeal was turned down, Stewart ran a publishing company and wrote books on natural childbirth and midwifery. In 1988, he became the director of the Central United States Earthquake Consortium, a group of earthquake-preparedness officials, and later that year he joined the faculty of Southeast Missouri State University. The next year, he became the director of the Center for Earthquake Studies. Three-quarters of his salary was paid by the university and the remainder by the Missouri Emergency Management Agency.

The evaluation of the Browning prediction and the news story about it had little impact. By that time, the earthquake seemed to have become an imperative. A friend of mine, a teacher in southern Missouri, told me, "I listen to my kids and their parents. They *want* an earthquake. They remember all that TV coverage of the one in San Francisco and it's almost as if they were saying, 'Hey, we could have one of those. Just like the big city. We could be on TV, and all.' " And by autumn many people and organizations had a stake in an earthquake, or at least the fear it generated. Sales of earthquake insurance jumped 50 percent, totaling $22 million in Missouri alone. A poll showed that half the population of the St. Louis area believed there would be an earthquake. Discount stores like Wal-Mart laid out displays of earthquake goods, taking as their guide special pull-out sections of newspapers across the region. Based on information from the Center for Earthquake Studies, these told what to do in an earthquake and what supplies to have available. The *Post-Dispatch* published a twenty-page earthquake-preparedness guide a week after it ran stories about the ad-hoc group's denigration of Browning's prediction and about Stewart's credentials. The section was stuffed with ads, including one for guns. The *Post-Dispatch* also ran a food-page special headed STOCKING AN EARTHQUAKE CUPBOARD. By late October, you could pick up your free copy of "Tremor Tips" in many public places, including schools. It came from Stewart's center and was Browning-friendly. It contained no ads but listed supplies necessary for riding out an earthquake and told how to prepare the house for one. The Red Cross issued information to smaller newspapers and distributed whistles to children in New Madrid to wear around their necks. Travel agencies in southeastern Missouri were promoting "earthquake getaway weekends," and so was the Convention and Visitors Bureau in Springfield, Missouri, some two hundred miles west of New Madrid. When NBC broadcast a two-part TV movie called *The Big One*, which wildly and deliciously distorted the destructiveness of earthquakes, Midwesterners gathered around their sets to watch, and their anxiety levels ratcheted upward. Critics accused NBC of bad timing, but its timing was nowhere near as bad as that of Missouri's Emergency Management Agency, which scheduled an earthquake drill, "Show Me Response '90," simulating the effects of a magnitude 7.6 earthquake, for 1 and 2 December. The drill would make use of emergency personnel statewide, including the National Guard, which would be flying Cobra attack helicopters. State officials insisted that the drill date was just a coincidence, but no one I knew believed that. Arkansas scheduled a similar drill on the same dates, and over in Tennessee plans were made to warehouse the dead and dying in a high-security prison in the western part of the state. The St. Louis area planned drills of its own for 2 December, directed from an underground command post, and enlisting the help of, among others, three sixteen-year-olds, who were assigned to struggle with firefighters after they were "rescued," and to scream, in order to contribute to "a general sense of panic," according to the newspaper report.

I left Washington after Thanksgiving to go back to Missouri. Arch Johnston, on hearing my plans, warned me that I would be in greater danger of harm driving between the two points than I would be in New Madrid on E Day. When I got to my farm, I felt as though I had stumbled into the countdown for Armageddon. Everywhere, I heard stories of people buying gas cans, batteries, even emergency power generators that cost thousands of dollars, stocking their pickups with emergency food and driving them out to the middle of their fields. I heard of white roses blooming blue out of season. The Mississippi River was said to be bubbling sulfur. A kindly, grandmotherly woman told me of the Bag 'Em and Tag 'Em Project: an "outfit" (unspecified) was said to have offered plastic bags and Magic Markers to the school in New Madrid so that overbusy undertakers could enlist the help of children to go out, pick up the dead, and label them as best they could. When I reacted with disgust and disbelief, she said, "Well, it *is* just awful, and they turned down the plastic bags. Took the Magic Markers, though." This was country cousin to a myth that floated around St. Louis earlier in the autumn—one about a major utility that was said to have ordered six thousand body bags with its name imprinted on them. And there were other rumors: the Disappearing Hitchhiker, that staple of modern myths, showed up in the Missouri bootheel, dressed in white, silent until he got out of a car; then he turned and said to the driver, "I'm here to warn you of the earthquake." Some reported that he was an angel. Blackbirds were said to be flying backward over the Mississippi River.

The Emergency Management Agency, which had originally been pleased to have the public's attention, admitted that it was overwhelmed. Its operations officer said, "I wish the panic had not gone along with the preparedness," and confessed that the office was now so overworked that it couldn't handle an emergency. The Earthquake Awareness Task Force announced that it had given out the wrong toll-free hot-line number, causing a travel agent (whose birthday was 3 December) in California no end of trouble.

The wonder was that anyone was immune to earthquake fever. But I heard wisecracks about the real disaster that was due to come on 4 December, when everyone poured out his bottled water. And a ten-year-old friend of mine gave me a rundown on her school's preparedness plans. The local school, unlike others, was steadfastly staying open on 3 December, but the children were being drilled, much to my informant's merriment. She giggled so hard she could barely speak when she told me about the kit given to each room with earthquake supplies in it, including a printed HELP sign that uninjured children were to throw out in the hallway to alert paramedics to the presence of wounded ones. The local director of emergency preparedness told me with disappointment that despite the fact that she'd put out collection cans, wrapped in yellow paper with a stunning black zigzag and labeled EARTHQUAKE DISASTER FUND, in seventeen places for five weeks, she'd collected only twelve dollars, and one can had been stolen. One Show-Me doubter had contributed two screws and a dead fly.

In an attempt to calm the populace, the state announced that Governor John Ashcroft, accompanied by Agriculture Director Charles Kruse (the man who had reluctantly given the O.K. for Browning to speak the year before), would tour the more interesting agricultural stops in the New Madrid area on 3 December.

Browning had once described what it would be like on 3 December. In the speech in which he supposedly forecast the San Francisco earthquake he also said that on 3 December 1990, "that high tide will be terrible . . . it will trigger volcanoes with the morning and evening suns, skies will glow pink."

On the morning of 3 December, under cloudy skies, I was awakened by my cat walking on my face. That was no unusual animal behavior presaging an earthquake. He does it every morning. As I fed him and groped for coffee, I remembered that I had to go to an earthquake. I arrived in New Madrid too late to witness the Illinois radio-station crew broadcasting live from the back table at Tom's Grill, but I heard that they had brought with them a 350-pound man and had him jump up and down to try to start the earthquake. News people filled the town. I counted fifty vehicles with satellite dishes and news logos, and then, like Dr. Robertson, who had counted the tremors of 1811–12, I got tired and quit. I looked local, so I was interviewed a lot. "Trouble is," one reporter told me, "everyone who is scared has left town and we can't get any good quotes from the ones who are here." The school had closed. Noranda Aluminum had promised a smoked turkey to any employee who showed up for work. I met the *Los Angeles Times* man. I heard about a reporter from a newspaper in Prague, Czechoslovakia. I looked in at Hap's Bar and Grill, which had begun a daylong Shake, Rattle, and Roll Party at 6:00 A.M. with beer and a bottomless pot of gumbo, and I could see no one who didn't look like a reporter. A young woman asked me to sign a notebook and tell where I was from. By noontime, she had two hundred signatures. By early afternoon, the museum was sold out of T-shirts. Inside the museum, I found a psychologist from California perched on a chair. He looked as though he were bustling even while sitting still. He had come to deal with "pretrauma stress in children," he told me, and he handed me his press kit. I asked him what he made of the Bag 'Em and Tag 'Em Project. He waved his hand dismissively. "Oh, that was *last* week's rumor," he said. "This week, it's extra embalming fluid for the mortuaries. These children are frightened. They'll tell you they aren't, but I know kids." He called a little girl over. "You know what to do in an earthquake?" he asked her, as he threw a yellow rubber duck up in the air. She stared at him. "What's that?" he prompted. "A duck?" she said. "That's right. Just duck," he said, laughing heartily, if singly. He pulled out a big, fuzzy green hand puppet. "This," he said in an aside to me, "is how we transform fear into anger." To the girl he said, "This is Iben Browning. Don't you want to punch him in the nose?" The little girl looked at him with incredulity and pity, that merciless gaze of childhood, and walked away.

Outside, although it was cold and windy, the town had taken on the air of a street party. Some nearby residents had driven into town to look at the media people and their equipment and preserve the scene on their own camcorders. Others stood in knots on street corners and were interviewed repeatedly. Some fought back. Lynn Bock, a town lawyer, strode into a restaurant and, peering through the viewfinder of his camcorder, pointed it at a table full of journalists. "O.K., everyone," he commanded. "Look right into the camera and, one by one, tell me who you are, where you're from, and who you work for." I watched journalists scuttle after Governor Ashcroft and Senator Christopher Bond, who had also shown up. And after a while I drove back home.

The New Madrid Seismic Zone was uncharacteristically quiet all that day, although there had been a magnitude 1 and a magnitude 2 the previous day. They were just routine, too small to be noticed except by seismographs. There were a few largish earthquakes recorded that day—5.0 to 5.5—but they were far away from any place Browning had mentioned in his predictions: New Caledonia, Tonga, and northern Colombia. And nowhere in the world during the five-day period he had allowed himself was there an earthquake of magnitude 6 or greater.

Iben Browning took his telephone off the hook.

There was one earthquake casualty. An eighty-two-year-old woman in Sparta, in south-central Missouri, following the directions in "Tremor Tips," had been removing breakables from a shelf and had fallen from a step stool and broken her hip.

A week later, David Stewart stepped down as director of the Center for Earthquake Studies and asked to be reassigned to full-time teaching.

A neighbor told me, "The next time some government feller tells me to fill up my pickup with peanut butter and drive it out into the middle of my field, I'm not a-gonna do it."

(February 1991)

ABOUT THE AUTHOR

SUE HUBBELL was born in Kalamazoo, Michigan. She splits her time between the Ozarks of southern Missouri, where she keeps bees, and Washington, D.C., where her husband works.

ABOUT THE TYPE

The text of this book was set in Janson, a
misnamed typeface designed in about 1690 by
Nicholas Kis, a Hungarian in Amsterdam. In
1919 the matrices became the property of the
Stempel Foundry in Frankfurt. It is an
old-style book face of excellent clarity and
sharpness. Janson serifs are concave and
splayed; the contrast between thick and thin
strokes is marked.